BEGIN WITH THE HEART

'Where then do we begin?' Meister Eckhart was asked.
'Begin with the heart'

Dedication
The Project is dedicated to those whose hearts are always beckoning them on; who put themselves in courageous conversation with the cliff-edge of their lives, no matter how frightening it seems

Daniel J. O'Leary

Begin with the Heart

RECOVERING THE SACRAMENTAL VISION

the columba press

First published in 2008 by
the columba press
55A Spruce Avenue, Stillorgan Industrial Park,
Blackrock, Co Dublin

Designed by Bill Bolger
Origination by The Columba Press
Printed in Ireland by ColourBooks Ltd, Dublin

ISBN 978-1-85607-611-1

Table of Contents

Acknowledgements

*Our deepest gratitude to those who participated in one or more week-end workshop(s)
2006-2008:*
Armitage, Mary: Leeds City Educational Advisor; Barralet, Roger OFM: Youth
Ministry; Bailey, Paula: Nottingham Diocese Education Service; Bolton, Marion:
Hallam Diocesan RE Centre; Byrne, Mary: Headteacher, Leeds Diocese; Darby,
Anne: Salford Diocese RE Centre; Doyle, Margaret: Salford Diocese RE Centre;
Groves, Bernie: Headteacher, Nottingham Diocese; Groves, Michael: Headteacher,
Nottingham Diocese; Huws Jones, Vanessa: General Adviser in Primary Education,
NYCC; Klein, Diana: Westminster Diocese Education and Formation Centre;
Laverick, Theresa: RE Advisor, Diocese of Hexham and Newcastle; Lunan, Jackie:
St John's RC Primary School; McAndrew, Michael: Dept for Evangelisation,
Clifton Diocese; McGrail, Peter: Liverpool Hope University; McDermott, Frank:
Schools and Formation, Hallam Diocese; McDermott, Sue: Anam Chara
Educational Support; McNamara, Sr Sheila: Newcastle Diocesan Primary Advisor
Marsh, Linda: Performance Manager, Leeds City Council; Mason, Denise: Parish
Catechist, Leeds Diocese; Mihilovic, Mary: Headteacher, Peterborough;
O'Donnell, Sharon: Adult RE Advisor, Hexham and Newcastle Diocese;
O'Riordan, Ken: Nottingham Diocese Education Services; Quigley, Joe: Catholic
Education Service (CES); Siberry, Margaret: CAFOD Director, Leeds Diocese;
Slavin, Willie: 'Networking' Journal; Stead, Kath: Council for Education,
Middlesbrough Diocese; Slingo, Tony; Parish Priest, Family Life Ministry,
Liverpool Archdiocese; Tippen, Kate: Nottingham Diocese Education Service.

*A very special thanks to the following for their expertise, guidance and immense support
during the years of preparing this Project:*
Hanvey, James SJ: Heythrop College, University of London; McDermott, Frank:
Hallam Diocese; Laverick, Theresa: Hexham and Newcastle Diocese; Mason,
Denise: ITQ Project Manager, N Yorks; Marsh, Linda: Performance Manager,
Leeds City Council; Siberry, Margaret: CAFOD Director, Leeds Diocese;
McAndrew, David: Former Director of Studies, St John's University, York;
Sullivan, John: Liverpool Hope University; Fagan, Sean SM: Author and Moral
Theologian; Kelly, Kevin; Parish Priest and Moral Theologian; Lillis, Margaret:
Shrewsbury Diocese Education Service; Antolic, Trish; Clifton Diocese RE Centre;
Rylands, Paddy: Shrewsbury Diocese Education Service; McCarthy, Cath: NHS
Manager; Smith, Shaun: Parish Priest, Hallam Diocese; Roberts, David: Paris
Priest, Shrewsbury Diocese Education Service; Gannon, Sr Nuala: Brentwood
Diocese RE Service; Mahon, David: 'Networking' Journal; Friel, Raymond;
Headteacher, Diocese of Clifton; Green, Brian: Parish Priest, Hallam Diocese;
Walsh, Patrick: Centre for Research in Catholic Education, University of London;
Wells, David: Department for Formation, Diocese of Plymouth.

In order of appearance, those who generously participated in creating the DVD:
Rohr, Richard; Hanvey, James; Siberry, Margaret; Marsh, Linda; Lythe, Patrice;
Freeman, Jill; Drought, Maureen; Burdekin, Peter; Clancy, Aidan; Vanier, Jean;
Jackson, Ashley; Scott, Wilma; Marsh, Selena; Marsh, Amber; Tulloch, Shirley;
Tulloch, Jonathan; Tulloch, Aidan; Grey, Mary.

Credits
Kairos Production Company
Demon Music Group (London) Public Domain Recordings
L'Arche (Canada)
Cathal Watters (additional camerawork)
Dermod McCarthy (RTÉ)
Simon Community (Leeds)

A big thank you to those who generously offered their professional skills in the final editing of the DVD:
Áine Moynihan, Eley McAinsh, Mary Colwell and Noel O'Briain.
Also to Richard Hayden and Graham Gallery of *Rejuvenateproductions* .

Executive Producer: Angela Graham
Producer/Director: Daniel O'Leary

Preface

There is no doubt that contemporary culture is both a challenge and an opportunity for women and men of faith. Faith cannot be simply a series of arguments defending propositions about God, Christ, the church, humanity and the world. It certainly needs a conceptual coherence which engages reason and imagination, but it needs something more. If all we are asked for is our intellectual assent, then faith remains largely formal and, to some extent, dead. Indeed, we can find many men and women who know all the arguments and counter arguments but still somehow faith remains elusive; at best, it never gets much beyond a routine of practices. If this is all there is, then I think once that supporting culture or community begins to dissolve or come under pressure then the 'faith' that it carries also begins to dissolve.

To be sure, faith is rooted and grounded in the community which it also creates. It is carried in the living tradition, the life of the church and in the holiness of its members. But it is also always a gift that comes new each day from the Spirit of the Risen Lord, the seal of the Father's love. The church lives each moment from this unfathomable and utterly free gift. Each day we come as beggars to receive the 'bread of life'. What is our prayer, whether personal or liturgical, if it is not the expression of our poverty?

In this we begin to touch something of faith's mystery. Beyond its conceptual structure it is always essentially a personal relationship. It comes as surprise and gift; it is not something that can be generated or produced; it is something offered and accepted. It is personal in the deepest and most direct way because it is Christ's offer of himself to each one, irrespective of their race, culture, status or ability. When we experience this, then, we know that it is also grace and we set out upon the adventure of this relationship which does not come to an end.

The adventure of faith does not take us out of the world but opens up a path that leads more deeply into it. How could it be anything else given that this is the path that God takes to come to us in the person and gift of his Son? And so we find ourselves on a road at once familiar but also strangely and inexplicably always new. It is the road of humanity itself and yet we find again and again that faith gives us a new way of seeing and understanding – a new way of being and maybe even opening up this way for others. This road is the way into that deeper relationship with Christ. It begins with the heart, but not the heart of a passing sentiment or emotion, rather, it is the heart that carries with it a sort of wisdom and courage, a sort of inventiveness also. This is the heart that is the school of the Spirit.

We find, too, that in this school we are not alone. We stand within a community that supports us and nourishes us, that helps us to stay on the journey, carrying us when we are weary or despondent, calling us when we lag behind or get distracted, inspiring with its own love and always holding before us the one who makes it all worthwhile.

The heart that lives in the school of the Spirit learns to discover a 'sacramental imagination'. It can express itself in many ways: in reason and poetry, in silence and in life – ordinary and heroic. That 'sacramental imagination' is the eye of the Christian heart which sees all things in Christ and traces the lines of his work – even in the darkest moments and the desert places. It has courage and it has truth; it is not some story of enchantment which the Christian invents as a sort of protective mantra against a hostile emptiness. It is truly the vision of faith because it sees God's faithfulness at work and knows how to wait upon him.

In his accessible and imaginative treatment, *Begin with the Heart*, Fr Daniel O'Leary has opened up the dimensions of this journey of the life of faith. He has also grounded it in a theological and ecclesial vision which brings out the personal, creative and dynamic reality which transforms not only our own life and understanding, but that of the culture in which we live. This book is about the mission we have to our culture and our world. It is also about how we, as parents, teachers, catechists, friends and companions can help unfold that life of faith in each other. That is truly a sacramental action. I have profited from reading Daniel's work and have learnt from his approach. I am grateful to him for taking up the suggestions of our report, *On The Way to Life*, and working with them sensitively and creatively. There is a lovely poem by e.e. cummings. It is not, I think, a religious poem but a love poem. Yet, its final stanza – which echoes Dante – has a resonance with all that is written in *Begin with the Heart*:

> here is the deepest secret nobody knows
> (here is the root of the root and the bud of the bud
> and the sky of the sky and the tree of a tree called life; which grows
> higher than the soul can hope or the mind can hide)
> and this the wonder that's keeping the stars apart
>
> i carry your heart (i carry it in my heart).

It is God who carries our heart in Christ, and in that wonderful exchange it is we who are given his through the love of the Holy Spirit. This seems to me to be the essence of the incarnation and the mystery of grace.

James Hanvey SJ
Director, The Heythrop Institute for Religion, Ethics and Public Life.

Introduction

These pages offer reflections for beginning a conversation about four inter-connected themes in the work of Christian education in its widest sense – the Catholic imagination and the sacramental vision (Part 1), a theology of nature and grace (Part 2), an educational theory for sharing our faith (Part 3), and the multi-cultural, postmodern reality of the world we live and work in (Part 4). These underlying motifs are central to *On the Way to Life* (OTWTL), a document commissioned by the Bishops of England and Wales in 2005 (see below).

All evangelising, catechising, teaching and preaching are based on a theology. It is important that we should be able to articulate it. Otherwise we do not have a ground to stand or build on. The Vatican II theology outlined in OTWTL is both imaginative and sacramental. It offers a vision of creation and incarnation that brings a new dynamism to our own faith and, therefore, to our ministry in the classroom and the parish-room.

Archbishop Vincent Nichols sees OTWTL as 'a vital catalyst for bishops, priests, teachers and all those involved in catechesis to reflect on the Church's mission in education.' What this document refers to as 'the Catholic imagination' and 'the sacramental vision' has always been an essential, but too often neglected, dimension of our tradition. It brings a richness and a resonance that gives new life to our efforts to spread the word.

Throughout the reflections that follow, suggestions are made for linking this sacramental imagination and theological vision with the actual lives of God's people, with pastoral ministries, and with an experience-based, life-centred educational theory. This is one of the hopes expressed by the Bishops' Conference, the Catholic Education Service (CES), and the authors and reviewers of OTWTL. They are concerned about how to maintain and enhance the spiritual integrity of Catholic schools in a 'results' dominated age.

Much creative work needs to be entered into before we can restore to the young and old of our schools and parishes this central spiritual vision and imagination. Many questions arise. How can hearts be touched?

How can faith be 'caught'? How do we protect and liberate that innate creativity already inside our students, waiting to be drawn out? How do we make both relevance to life and abundance of humanity the aim of all our teaching and catechising? How do we keep the vision of Jesus at the heart of everything we do?

One way is by paying more attention to the hearts and minds of those who work so generously and faithfully in our parishes and schools. Too often the prescribed books and programmes do not touch the source of all transformation – the spirit, enthusiasm and motivation of the educator. The heart of catechesis is the heart of the catechist. The teacher's spirit must be transformed before the students' will be. 'Unless the faith means something to the teacher,' Cardinal Hume used to say, 'it will not mean much to the student.'

Another way of keeping Christ at the centre is by restoring to people once again what belongs to them, by virtue of their birth and baptism – that is, their idealistic fire, their divine light and unique loveliness. Maybe we need, as Ronald Rolheiser holds, to re-romanticise faith, religion and church; to give our students something beautiful to fall in love with, as John Paul II insisted. One thing needs to be noted. Given the continually changing nature of the world we live in, a mere adaptation of what worked in the past may not be enough.

Maybe another renaissance is needed – a renaissance of the sacramental imagination. The use of those words should not put us off. Imagination, sacramentality and faith have always been sisters. Imagination is the divine creativity within us. The way we faithfully co-create our lives and the world with God depends on the vitality of our imagination and Catholic vision. Such imaginative vision needs to be nourished through exposure to the arts, to the great stories of the world, to intimate conversations with ourselves and with others, to play and to children, to poetry and to music, and to everything that nurtures our intuition and our sensitivity to God's presence all around us. (This is the focus of the attached DVD.) Part of the challenge of this task is always to be true to the central place of the familiar and traditional dimensions we rely on for the definition and sharing of the Catholic faith.

We have, of course, been here, or close to here, before. Throughout these pages the reader will notice many references to the post-Vatican II decades when much devoted work was entered into by the churches in these countries and elsewhere so as to clarify, cultivate and nurture new shoots of promise in the world of Christian education. The Bishops' Conference Report *On the Threshold* (2000) was a striking example of such promising work. Many church leaders in education believe that now is the time for another renewed and courageous beginning.

To meet the daunting challenges of today's complex society (Part 4) we need good creative theology and dedicated teaching. While holding fast to the fullness of our tradition, we need to set free the Catholic imagination and sacramental vision that has always characterised that tradition. Without catching the vision, the heart does not know where to go; but without the fire of imagination it doesn't want to go anywhere, least of all to church!

As teachers and catechists we are called to work with a passion for acquiring that central vision in ourselves, first. We must, in fact, *become* the vision. Filled with that vision, and together with a clear awareness of our complex cultures, we can all be part of a new and blessed renaissance in our church and world.

Notes

These reflections, drawn in large part from *On the Way to Life*, are meant for all facilitators involved with any age-group in evangelising, catechising, forming, religiously educating and preaching in the Catholic tradition of Christianity. Throughout, the term 'students' is used to include all those (pupils, teenagers, adults) who participate in such educational ministries in school and parish.

On The Way to Life: Contemporary Culture and Theological Development as a Framework for Catholic Education, Catechesis and Formation. A Study prepared by the Heythrop Institute for Religion, Ethics and Public Life and commissioned by the Department for Education and Formation of the Bishops' Conference for England and Wales. The Catholic Education Service (CES) is facilitating its dissemination. While readers may wish to read the full text of the document at a later date, there is no need to have done so before exploring *Begin with the Heart*.

Part One will have a special interest for readers who seek a deeper understanding of the notion of the Catholic imagination that lies at the heart of this book and of the author's other books.

Part Two sets out to explain and explore the attraction of the traditional theology of nature and grace that radically changes our understanding and experience of 'the abundant life'.

Part Three focuses more particularly on the implications of this theology and vision for teaching, catechising, preaching and the exercise of all church ministries.

Part Four briefly addresses the challenges of 'telling our story' in a richly multi-cultural, postmodern society.

If you find yourself at sea from time to time in the following pages, just skip on to the next sentence or paragraph and you will sail again on familiar waters. The format of the material in these pages is cyclical; there is a repetition in the structure that keeps coming back to the central theme.

The DVD is best watched after Part Two.

The title and sub-title of each of the four Parts is followed by a sequence of quotations to stimulate thinking. This is followed by a brief preview of the contents of that particular Part. Each Part is rounded off by a short summary of the Sections and a series of discussion points. A brief glossary is added at the end.

Part One

Gifts of Imagination

On the Way to Life (OTWTL) is like a coat of many colours, and we are all attracted to our favourite hue within it. Many commentators and reviewers have indicated their preference for this or that theme, praising its promise for a deeper understanding of our current catechesis, teaching and formation. What captured the attention of many was the excitement and rich potential of what the authors call 'the Catholic Imagination'. They offer it as a grounding for renewing the process of effective catechesis in a world and in a culture that is forever changing. 'This would mean developing the sacramental imagination with the theology of nature and grace that underpins it, as the core conceptual structure for all the cognitive elements of educational and formational programmes. It would help to create a structural coherence between family, parish and school' (p 67). It is well worth reflecting on this exceptionally strong statement. It carries, as well, implications for other pastoral initiatives in the home countries. What follows is an attempt to unpack it.

The world needs the unifying power of the imagination.
R. S. Thomas

Imagination is more important than knowledge.
Albert Einstein

The human faculty of imagination is one of the most neglected and most misunderstood areas within contemporary theology ... Imagination is, as it were, a bridge between human experience, understanding and interpretation. It is the imagination that enables human understanding to take place and it is impossible for understanding to exist without the power of imagination.
Dermot A. Lane

You may not consider it blasphemy, I hope, that belief in God depends on the direction of our imagination. You will know that the imagination is the highest and most original element in us.
Friedrich Schleiermacher

With imagination you don't have to travel far to find God – only notice things. The finite and the infinite live in the same place. It is here alone, at this precarious and vital point, that the holy secret is laid bare. 'I live in this world by attention.'
Simone Weil

For what is a man's heart but his imagination.
George Bernard Shaw

The aim of the artist is to render the highest possible justice to the visible universe ... The artist penetrates the concrete world in order to find at its depths the image of its source, the image of ultimate reality.
Flannery O'Connor

The concept of sacramentality must be broken open so that we rediscover the sacramental potential of all creation. In such a vision the Eucharist becomes a focal point that is inclusive rather than exclusive in its capacity to express and celebrate the abundant sacramentality of everyday life, in which the surplus of meaning spills over into society, culture and indeed the cosmos itself, so that it cannot be contained in structures, rules and institutions.
Tina Beattie

The only real fall of man is his non-eucharistic life in a non-eucharistic world.
Alexander Schmemann

Reclaiming Imagination –
The Forgotten Dimension

This first section indicates that together with creativity, inspiration and beauty, imagination too must be found at the heart of our Catholic faith and education. It introduces the role of imagination in the work of catechesis and teaching. As with our consideration of theology in Part Two, we have to ease ourselves into a familiarity with this concept. We need to be reminded that already deeply embedded in faith and its practices, is the gift of imagination. To avoid confusion for the reader, terms such as 'theology of nature and grace', 'sacramental vision' and 'the Catholic imagination' are all, in the present context, intrinsically connected.

Hard on the heels of the general euphoria of the sixties in general, and of the Second Vatican Council, in particular, waves of fresh hope, and dreams of new beginnings were flowing across the land. Those of us who were young teachers and priests at that time were full of energy and excitement. Truly incarnational theology, liturgical openness and catechetical imagination were filling our days and nights. There would be a transformed church soon, where teaching, parenting and preaching would be realistic and optimistic, challenging and fulfilling, where human wholeness and holiness would be essentially compatible.

With heart and soul we entered into this brave new world of the seventies and eighties, living the questions and exploring the seemingly unlimited potential for growth and vision. In the world of catechesis and religious education, writers and theologians such as Karl Rahner, Enda McDonagh and Kevin Nichols, educationalists such as David Konstant, Christianne Brusselmans and Patrick Purnell, institutions such as Louvain in Belgium, Dundalk in Ireland and Corpus Christi College in the UK, were all deeply devoted to finding dynamic ways forward.

But something happened to the creative promise of those post-Council days. Fears surfaced, cautions followed, rival approaches were championed. During those decades of doubt, enthusiasm faded and a certain vision was almost lost. But not completely, and only for a while. God always sends us what we need – eventually. In spite of a perceived lack of nourishment over the years, the green shoots of Vatican II have never died. They still keep appearing. There is one in particular that brings much hope.

Many reviewers of *On the Way to Life* (OTWTL – see Introduction), have indicated their preference for this or that theme within it, praising its promise of a deeper understanding of our current catechesis, teaching and formation. What captured the attention of many was the rich potential of what the authors call 'the Catholic imagination'. They offer it as a grounding for renewing the process of effective catechesis in a church that is losing ground in a world-culture that is forever changing. 'This would mean developing the sacramental imagination with the theology of nature and grace that underpins it, as the core conceptual structure for all the cognitive elements of educational and formational programmes. It would help to create a structural coherence between family, parish and school.' It is well worth reflecting on this strong statement which, of course, refers to all kinds of adult formation too. What follows is an attempt to unpack it.

In *Retrieving Imagination in Theology*, Michael Paul Gallagher reminds us of Schleiermacher's comment about belief in God depending on the direction of our imagination, the highest and most original element in us. He offers ample evidence of the respected place that the gift of imagination holds in the theologies of John Henry Newman, Karl Rahner, Hans Urs von Balthasar and Bernard Lonergan. Rejecting a strait-jacket type of doctrinal formulation, these theologians gravitate, he writes, to the uses of imagination for liberating us into a deeper awareness and experience of the mystery of Incarnation. 'Theology needs to approach art and literature more as experience than as message or meaning. The wavelength shared by theology and imagination lies in the whole adventure and joy of self-transcendence in its many forms.'[1]

the Catholic imagination

It is not easy to define 'the Catholic imagination'. It has to do with a wonderful capacity for seeing into, and beyond, the mystery of what happens. It allows us first to experience what is presented to us, and then to discover within it, much more meaning than the basic phenomena would allow. In one of his weekly columns, Ronald Rolheiser quotes from W. Wright's *Sacred Heart, Gateway to God:* 'A layered reality is part of the Catholic imagination. To possess this imagination is to dwell in a universe inhabited by unseen presences – the presence of God, the presence of the saints, the presence of one another. This life transcends the confines of space and time.'[2]

Rolheiser goes on to draw attention to what is all but lost today, namely the fact that reality is more than just physical, that it has layers that we do not perceive empirically, that there is more mystery within ordinary life than can be measured. We live in a world that is 'mystically tone-deaf, where all the goods are in the shop window'. The mystical imagination is not only as real as the scientific imagination; it reveals what science, on its own, could never tumble to – the many grace-drenched and spirit-laden layers of reality, even inside the law of gravity, that are not always readily available to the senses.

We can build up a picture of what is meant by 'the Catholic imagination' from the references and comments made in its regard by the authors of OTWTL. They write about a 'sacramentality' that is inclusive, mystical, incarnational, and that has a coherent 'central vision'. There is 'a desire in every human heart' for transcendence. We are all on 'a search for God' since our 'human nature is intrinsically ordered to God'. It is this that makes us so wonderfully human. This 'profound Catholic intuition, in which grace is seen as constitutive of human nature, transforms our understanding both of Revelation and of our humanity.'

We are on the brink, here, I think, of being one step closer to how OTWTL might enrich the theory and practice of parish catechesis and school ethos.

> 'If grace is integral to nature, then all nature in some way has the capacity to disclose grace and be a vehicle for it.'[3]

That sentence, from a life-enhancing theology of nature and grace, has within it, the quiet power to transform the very basis of our teaching, pastoral ministry and preaching. 'It opens the possibility of an enriched spirituality (that) allows people to understand the sacramental nature of their ordinary lives ...' Everyone then, particularly teachers in the widest sense of that calling, becomes 'a minister of grace (with) the possibility of mediating it in, and through, their lives.'[4]

If we reflect on these profound statements, and let our imagination run with them, then some fairly far-reaching questions will arise – about, for instance, what we think we're doing with RCIA enquirers, First Sacraments candidates and their parents, and almost all education within home, school and parish. Now many of the OTWTL statements we already know. So why the fuss? Well, because there are levels of knowing. Not all knowing captures the imagination and sets our hearts on fire. There is a knowing that burns within us and becomes a wisdom that yearns to be shared.

When we reflect on the central emphasis of the document with an open mind, we find an intensity about the way it lifts humanity, and all things created, into new levels of meaning. They now become the locus of revelation.

> There is a theology of creation and incarnation that, in solidarity with Christ, the Human One, focuses on this world, and everything in it, as the continuing presence of the divine.

The document retrieves and honours an orthodox tradition that, for one reason or another, had almost been lost and has been sorely missed. It explores 'a Catholic humanism (with its) deep and rich history from the Fathers into the nineteenth and twentieth centuries, finding its expression both theologically and practically in the mystical traditions of the church'.[5] The task, then, is to become more human, not less; to love the world more, not less.

There is much to reflect on in John Paul's hopes for today's world and church. 'What is needed,' he wrote, 'are ministers of the gospel who are experts in humanity, familiar with their own emotions and able to share them with others, and who are, at the same time, contemplatives who have fallen in love with God.' It takes immense imagination to take the incarnation literally, to identify God's signature on everything around us, to see God's face behind every face, to discover the Lover-God who comes to us disguised as our lives.

Reclaiming Beauty

When Albert Einstein holds that imagination is more important than knowledge, and when George Bernard Shaw equates the language of the heart with imagination, perhaps it is the notion of creativity, openness and beauty that they are trying to protect. Beauty and imagination are too often obscured by the high walls of logic. Formulations and doctrines will never do justice to mystery. Faith is more than the sum of its constituent beliefs. It is a way of imagining and experiencing our divine/human world. That is why, after the narrowness of modernist critiquing, prophets in the church are trying to recover the neglected role of imagination, the 'poetics of theology' and its artistic expression, in the more positive and open approach of the contemporary human spirit.

We all have within us the icon of God, the source of beauty. No less an authority than Thomas Aquinas has written: 'God puts into creatures,

along with a kind of sheen, a reflection of God's own luminous ray ...
From this Beautiful One, beauty comes to be in all beings ...' Hans Urs
Von Balthasar, too, believes that at the deepest level of our being, we
already 'vibrate sympathetically' with beauty because we ourselves are
beautifully created. In its presence, he says, we fall into 'aesthetic arrest'.
He sees beauty and grace as one. It disturbs us, captivates us, provokes
us. It keeps our eyes on distant horizons of ultimate beauty. It is what
keeps us searching for God.[6]

God the source of
beauty

Many readers will be aware of the devotion to beauty expressed in the
writings of St Augustine, Dietrich Bonhoeffer and Simone Weil. We
love reading the clear, pure expressions of beauty in the meditations of
the mystics of the past and present.

| With imagination you don't have to travel far to find God – only
| notice things. The finite and the infinite live in the same place.
It is here alone, at this precarious and vital point, that the holy secret is
laid bare. God walks in two shoes – the shoe of creation and the shoe of
incarnation. Each footfall is a threshold moment – the breath before the
vision, the cusp between the seen and the unseen, the substance of
things hoped for, evidence of the invisible. 'I live in this world by attention', wrote Simone Weil.

How can beauty, this powerful sacrament of the incarnate God, be
somehow harnessed in the service of our evangelising, catechising and
teaching? The authors of OTWTL enlist the power of beauty in their
quest for the reclaiming of the Catholic imagination. They want to
restore its pride of place in our teaching and preaching. 'The practice of
faith in all its forms is the participation in the beauty that God is, and it
is the constant disclosure of that beauty in the world. Thus art, in all its
modes, is not something that is a luxury, but the very living out of the
vision of God. For this reason, the aesthetic of the life of faith is integral to the sacramental vision and it is also integral to religious education,
catechesis and formation ...'[7]

This powerful statement is asserting that when we truly believe, we are
both participating in, and revealing, God's beauty.

| All artistic enterprise is a part of this epiphany.
The statement is a call to a greater appreciation of the beautiful in the
practice and teaching of our faith.

In one of his first homilies as Pope, Benedict XVI said: 'If the church is
to transform and to humanise the world, how can she dispense with
beauty in her liturgies; that beauty which is so closely linked with love,
and with the radiance of the Resurrection' and at the end of Vatican II,

Pope Paul VI had a tribute paid to artists of all kinds, which included these words: 'The church needs you and turns to you. The world we live in needs beauty in order not to rush into despair … It is beauty, like truth, which makes the invisible world palpable, and brings joy to the human heart.' These papal sentiments come straight from a Catholic sacramental imagination.

Small wonder the authors call for the support of artists, musicians, poets and dancers in the clarification and presentation of their vision. It is a truly enchanting one, deeply contemplative, and teeming with pedagogical possibilities. It is not fearful of appealing to the senses, nor does it deny the holistic and poetic nature of the precious ministry of handing on the faith. It has no reason to. In its mystical tradition, Catholicism is notoriously sacramental, and a champion of beauty. St Thomas Aquinas, again, refers to 'a kind of sheen of divine loveliness' that all creatures carry. Hans Urs von Balthasar, too, reminds us that without a feeling for beauty we cannot pray, 'and soon, will no longer be able to love.'

> Whether in teaching or preaching the privilege of the teacher or preacher is to reveal the presence of God's beauty already there in what is happening all around.

beauty awakens the divinity within us

How rarely we teach, catechise or preach about beauty! The life-centred themes and topics of the various syllabuses we use are there to be mined for the holy treasure of beauty and form that they often carry in disguise. And beauty always invites, enchants and awakens the sleeping divinity within us. The authors of the document put it well: 'The theology of grace that informs Vatican II recovers "the ordinary" as the realm of grace, God's "better beauty"; hence the aesthetic of holiness is not something exceptional but the same thing that is shaped in the realm of the domestic, giving to it, the weight of glory; the alchemist's stone is Christ.'[8]

Catholic Sacramentality

Teaching about the sacraments takes up a huge amount of all catechesis, formation, preaching and religious education. The liturgy in all its variations is rightly at the centre of our faith. Many fear that bland repetition and a cautious 'rubrical mentality', are gradually draining the life-blood from our celebrations. There is a vitality in the insights of OTWTL that could bring a fresh enthusiasm into our often-jaded ways of catechising about, and celebrating, the liturgy in school and parish.

The authors ask us to understand the liturgy in terms of the revealing and clarifying of God's healing presence in the substance of our lives. 'The liturgy is the routine inscription of eternity in time, the continual action of Christ who is Lord of time ... In the liturgy the "ordinary" is consecrated and made the place of divine encounter. By its very "routine" and "ordinariness" the liturgy writes us into time; in its rhythms and seasons it celebrates our finitude and embodiedness. It is not an escape to eternity from the contradictions of our finite temporal existence, but a way of seeing them within the greater horizons of God's eternal life.'[9]

With assured words and images, OTWTL places an awareness of human experience at the heart of God's self-disclosure. Our privileged task is to consecrate the ordinary, to draw out from its womb, like midwives of mystery, the embodied presence of our wonderful God. 'RE, catechesis and formation must also be attentive to the mystery at the heart of the world and of all human life. That means that we need to have confidence in our theology of nature and grace. It is essentially a theology that makes explicit the "eternity in the heart" of every human person which is constantly seeking expression and form. The Catholic sacramental vision is the sacrament of the human heart as well and cannot help but find a deep resonance there.'[10]

Consecrating the ordinary

There is no dualism in true sacramentality. The radical distinction between the sacred and the profane has been overcome in the person of Christ. In him it is revealed that the locus of the divine is now the human. We celebrate the liturgy of our daily lives so as to fruitfully celebrate the liturgy of the church. Christian liturgy is the memory and celebration of the deepest dimension of human life, namely, the self-communicating power and beauty of the indwelling Blessed Trinity. The sacraments do not confer a grace that was absent until then. Sacraments proclaim and enable us to own a love that is already the core of our being. They exist to restore the world to its true nature. 'Not only does grace build on nature, but this relationship grounds human freedom, and thus, the possibilities that nature has for realising itself.'[11]

It all begins with God. God's imagination is the key to who we are.
All human imagination is a reflection of the divine imagination.
It is, as W. B. Yeats put it, 'our evidence of God'. Divine imagination is wider and wilder than we could ever dream of; and it is closer and more loving than we dare hope. God's imagination is at work in every aspect of creation from the heart of the cosmos to the heart of the tiniest insect, and in the very core of our own being.

We sense the divine creativity, in a most intimate way, in our own deepest desire – the desire to create, to be radically original, to break through our limitations, to fulfil God's dream in us, to become full of divine light. We reflect the imagination of God in our passion for the possible, in our everlasting hope even when all seems lost. Beyond a knowledge of God, and of conditioned religious behaviour, it is in our existential longing for the experience of God that imagination is fully at play.

God's imagination in us calls us to be faithful to our own originality. It is invincible, uncontrollable and essentially free because it carries no fear. It is eminently trustable. It can live with paradox, difference and contradiction. It does not come with programmes for procedure or instructions for completion. It is about possibility. 'I dwell in possibility' wrote Elizabeth Barrett Browning. So must we. In his inaugural speech in 1994, Nelson Mandela suggested that it was not our frailty, faults and failures that held us back; it was, he said, our inner glory and shining beauty that terrifies us. God sets no limits. We do. And usually because we're afraid.

God's imagination in us calls us to be faithful to our own originality.

Into the Future

The reclaiming of what is meant by 'the Catholic imagination' presents a great challenge to all of us. A precious, unique but neglected Catholic tradition of Christian humanism is waiting to be explored. This exploration will be more than a cerebral one. Basic knowledge of the poetry of imagination and sacramentality is not enough. Intellectual perception is a second-order reflection. The true understanding that lasts and transforms depends on the intensity of the actual experience of what is known. There is a daunting challenge here. It takes imagination to craft a new creation between the knowledge of the head and the intuition of the heart.

The sacramental imagination and actual experience

Writing about 'sacramental abundance', David Power asks, 'How can we, in a time of computerisation and remote control, get beyond the stranglehold that technique and concept have on language, so that it may speak "in, with, and under" bread, wine, oil and water, through a poetics that allows the things themselves to come to speech, and through them, the gift of divine love and divine life that Jesus and the Spirit have poured into them?'[12]

Some OTWTL commentators have suggested placing a greater trust in the imagination of our teachers and catechists, with less anxiety about detailed scripts and complicated structures, and more scope for improvisation in the sharing of gospel values within the culture of our time. A great part of the unfolding of the current project may well be the task of setting the hearts of the teachers and catechists on fire with a deeper grasp of the astonishing beauty of the good news they are sharing, and then, whatever the syllabus or programme, the listeners will catch the excitement of the teacher. Maybe it is time to encourage our well-informed teachers to trust more confidently in their own imagination already full of God's creativity.

The greatest threat to the rooting and blossoming of OTWTL will, I fear, be a lack of this very imagination on our part. Many of us still carry the memory of the way we were. A few years ago the Irish poet Seamus Heaney spoke about the loss of our imaginative perspective on the world arising from economic and social change: 'I would say that the more important Catholic thing is the actual sense of eternal values and infamous vices which our education or formation gives us. There's a sense of profoundness, a sense that the universe can be ashimmer with something, and Catholicism was the backdrop to the whole thing. The world I grew up in offered me a sense that I was a citizen of the empyrean – the crystalline elsewhere of the world. I think that's gone from Catholicism now.'[13]

But maybe not for long more. Maybe John Paul II's millennium dreams for 'a new springtime' in the church are beginning to come true.

Summary

Catholicism is notoriously sacramental; it champions imagination.

The 'sacramental vision' has a central place in Catholic education.

There is a kind of knowing that excites the heart, which 'is commonly reached, not through reason, but through the imagination.' (Cardinal John H. Newman)

Faith is a way of imagining our world as made in God's image.

'Imagination is necessary for faith.' (Robert Haight) 'According to our mystical theologians it is only through the imagination that the presence of the spiritual world is evoked and invoked. Its context is contemplation.' (David Roberts)

There is a need to recover the place of beauty in our catechesis.

All human imagination is a reflection of God's imagination: it is the cradle of possibility.

It takes imagination to hold together the knowledge of the head and the intuition of the heart. We need the unifying power of imagination.

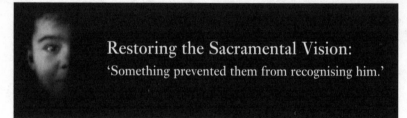

Restoring the Sacramental Vision:
'Something prevented them from recognising him.'

One of the themes of this section is about nurturing and releasing the divine imagination incarnate in all students. Too often the creativity of children and adults is suppressed by inadequate catechesis. Without the sacramental vision it is impossible to recognise the presence of God all around. The task of the educator is, beyond the giving of new information to students, to bring them to the edge of their own divine possibilities for recognising the divine everywhere. Story, poetry and all the creative arts become a necessary part of this adventure. A basic aim is to provide space for graced vision to happen. This chapter makes some preliminary comments on the implications for teaching and catechising arising from the core message of OTWTL – about the church's work in spreading the gospel, in handing on the faith, in making Christianity real for the people of today's world.

A s the credits roll at the end of *The Lion, the Witch and the Wardrobe*, Lucy doubts whether the whole amazing experience could ever happen again. Yes, it can, she is assured, but only if you keep your eyes open. It is the ordinary that contains the mystery, not the extraordinary. In another work, *Till We Have Faces*, C. S. Lewis tries to show how human love only blossoms when its divine sap is alive within it. The journey is not away from routine events, it is into the heart of things. Who would have ever imagined that the way to wonder could run through an old wardrobe! Without imagination our travels will be brief.

Stories precede doctrine

Every good story tells a deeper one. Whether it be one of the Narnia Chronicles, or the home-spun tale of local life, the story is a powerful way of dealing with life-giving mysteries. In the beginning was the story. It was there when we were small. It was there before the doctrines of the religions were formulated. It was there before the gospels were written.

It was there before anything was written. And it still has not lost its imaginative power to open hearts and minds to the wonder of life.

And the same is true of all the artists who are dedicated to the spreading of beauty. It is the work of the artist to reveal the secrets of the every-day, to release the music of what happens. The artist surrenders herself to the wider worlds of meaning, allowing herself to be drawn beyond the immediate. For her, normal life is full of 'hints and guesses' about another reality; experiences that are, as Lewis reminds us, 'only the scent of a flower we have not found, the echo of a tune we have not heard, news from a country we have never yet visited.'

> It is the work of the artist to reveal the secrets of the every-day, to release the music of what happens.

To know something more completely we need to appreciate it in its fullness and in our wholeness. There is a way in which the dance, the drama, the song, the music, the painting touch us profoundly. Wonderful as words are, they are quite limited when it comes to the sharing of mystery. The *Logos* stands for more than words alone can say. Realising the profundity of the implications of Revelation for young and old, the authors of OTWTL call in the support of the artists, in the awesome task of spreading this word.

Windows of Wonder

Basically, the Catholic sacramental imagination is an effort to recover a revealed insight about the meaning of the incarnation. That insight concerns the actual enfleshing of God's own self, first in Jesus, and, because of our solidarity with him, in all of us as well. It would look to our humanity and to our human experiences as the prime site, so to speak, for the unfolding of, and for our encounter with, the incarnate presence of God. It is so important to believe that God is in no way diminished when nature and humanity are revealed as potentially divine.

That we are created in God's image is a truth to be assimilated in different ways, at different levels, through many media – and slowly throughout our lives. It is too wondrous to believe that we are living co-creators of divine beauty, blessed with extraordinary power and grace. Here are a few more brief reminders and pointers to those truths. St Simeon wrote: 'These hands of mine are the hands of God; this body of mine is the body of God because of the incarnation.' The mystic Meister Eckhart preached: 'You are God's seed. As the pear seed grows into the pear tree and the hazel seed becomes the hazel tree, so does God's seed in you become God.' St Andrew reminds us in the Office of Readings for Our Lady's birthday, that the Word-made-flesh is 'the unveiling of the mystery ... and the deification of human nature assumed by God.' The language of St Thomas is disturbingly forth-right. Creation was not radically re-adjusted in the incarnation, he held; rather was it essentially completed in Christ. 'The incarnation accomplished this, that God became human and that human beings became God ...' Running through the streets of Genoa, St Catherine startled the shoppers by shouting with delight 'My deepest me is God!'

The poets and artists, the mystics and contemplatives, are never tired of exploring this dimension of the mystery. For them the smallest particle of creation becomes a window on God's beauty. They see eternity in the grain of sand and infinity in an hour. Their intense energy is spent on revealing how the world is charged with the grandeur of God. They forever use images and symbols to catch the fire-fly glimpses of the extraordinary presence of the Spirit of Wonder beneath the seemingly superficial and ordinary. The work of the true teacher, too, they point out, is to notice the seeds of sacramentality scattered all around.

We can only teach it, and hear it, with immense reverence and joy. And the wise teacher will remember that there will always be 'something preventing us from recognising him' – strong feelings, to do with original sin, of resistance and anxiety around such holy work. There is no dualism here. In a truly incarnational theology of creation, nature and grace are not side by side, or over against each other. The one is the context for the other. Neither is diminished by the other: they both complete each other.

Nature and grace complement each other.

In the DVD that accompanies OTWTL James Hanvey, the main author of the report, gives us a lovely image about the moment when Christianity meets a post-modern culture, when grace meets nature, when, in meditation, we contemplate our lives in the light of Revelation. Take culture, nature, our human experiences as a song, not pitch-perfect, not quite finished, still slightly unsure of itself. Revealed grace approaches humbly and respectfully. It does not criticise or suggest a better tune. Instead, it begins to hum along, gradually introducing a little harmony here, a descant there, a shift in emphasis at times – all enriching and enhancing the original melody. In the interests of clarity, purity and beauty, it suggests some adjustments, a few omissions, some inclusions. Together, the piece is finally set to music, perfecting and revealing the truth of what was in both nature and grace from the beginning – but a truth that needed both realities to co-create its true splendour.

And so sacramental vision is achieved, not just with new spectacles, but by new eyes. It embraces what is there, and intensifies its meaning. It celebrates reality, and exposes its true nature. It diminishes nothing, only enhances everything. It reveals the meaning below the meaning, the beauty behind the beauty, the mystery within the mystery. The basic, faded image of God is cleaned up and revealed in its original colours; a profound spiritual dimension is rediscovered within the often-shallow surface of life. This kind of startling vision has many implications for our schools and parishes. The authors of OTWTL are right to suggest that a paradigm shift in our approaches to catechesis and formation will be needed once the Catholic imagination is restored to its rightful place in our faith.

Unfamiliar perhaps at first, the day may come when we finally begin to understand, at the depths of our being, like second nature, that the human is the threshold to the reality of God. 'The gateway to heaven is everywhere' wrote St Catherine of Sienna. As St John Chrysostom put it, 'Seek the key that unlocks the human heart; the same key opens the heart of God.' 'Salvation', the Church Fathers remind us, 'hinges on the flesh.' From now on, our attention and our focus will be trained on recognising the God of surprises hiding and playing at the heart of life.

The human is the threshold to the reality of God

And there are many delightful theological insights to be explored. John Paul II referred to this 'theology of creation' in his *Tertio Millennio Adveniente* letter welcoming in the new millennium. And his poetry teems with a spirituality and imagery that spring from such a theology which is more of a love-story about original joy than a lament about original sin.[14] Long before any Fall, the Word was already gladly becoming flesh in the first creation. 'God is sheer joy', proclaimed Thomas Aquinas, 'and sheer joy demands company.'

Aquinas praised 'bigness' (magnanimity) as a mirror of God. 'Deliberate stinginess' (pusillanimity) he described as sin.

> Systems based on fear and bad teaching will try to desiccate our souls and rob us of our divine essence.

They draw the boundaries closer. Appealing only to our ego and insecurity, they fill the open spaces with danger and threat. It takes courageous imagination to keep the bigger picture in focus, to keep lifting and rolling the stone away, to keep waiting for the veils to part and reveal the deeper realities. Otherwise we become the victims of everything that dams up and blocks those wild and free flowings and blowings of the Holy Spirit. And that is why we need our teachers and catechists to be liberated into a deeper and vibrant vision of their graced vocation.

The pastoral ministers in our schools and parishes have, especially over the last few decades, sought a better grounding in the kind of theology which OTWTL advocates. It will be a major task for our leaders to organise such a necessary service if we hope for a significant breakthrough in our teaching, catechising and preaching.

In the introduction to *Evaluating the Distinctive Nature of a Catholic School* (CES 1994) we are reminded that 'Everything connected with human living, and the means by which we understand and come to terms with it, is part of God's self-revelation to humanity, whether those engaged in it are conscious of it or not. Despite our sinfulness or shortcomings, every person's life is charged with God's presence, and every human experience presents us with the opportunity to deepen our knowledge and love of him ... The whole of creation is God's gift to us and through the incarnation, takes on the characteristics of the sacred.'

Everything is part of God's self-revelation.

In the same document (A-2) we read, 'Every human life is filled with God's presence. Christ's incarnation has changed the world, making of God's good creation a sacramental means by which he reveals himself to us ... Those involved in the school's life may thus experience, through-out every moment of the day, that God is at the centre of the learning process and is the ultimate goal of the curriculum.

> Although it may be convenient to speak of the 'religious' cur-riculum and 'secular' curriculum in the Catholic school, as though these were separate and distinct, in reality, the curricu-lum as a whole, and every part of it, is religious, since there is nothing which does not ultimately relate to God.'

There are also glimpses and reflections of a Catholic sacramental vision in the first introduction to our National Primary Syllabus: 'Teachers, like parents, have a special role as co-creators with God, to enable others to be, in their turn, co-creators with God too.' 'Our human experience is the medium through which revelation takes place.' 'There cannot be two parallel lives in our existence – on the one hand the so-called spirit-ual life and on the other, the so-called secular life.' 'Only in the unfold-ing of our lives is the eternal plan of God revealed in each one of us ... Every area of our lives enters into the plan of God, who desires that these very areas be the place where the love of Christ is revealed and realised.'

This initial promise, however, in some syllabuses, seems to get lost in its actual practical application. The structure and sequence of the method-ology often seem to favour knowledge over wisdom, information over transformation. It is one thing for the teacher or student to know and remember necessary knowledge; it is entirely another thing to ingest and to enflesh it so thoroughly that it becomes the very essence of every-thing that is taught and learnt. William Cowper wrote,

> Knowledge and wisdom, far from being one,
> have oft-times no connection. Knowledge dwells
> in heads replete with thoughts of other men;
> wisdom in minds attentive to their own.

Knowledge is proud that he has learned so much.
Wisdom is humble that he knows no more.[15]

This interface between knowledge and wisdom, between learning about the faith and catching its vision, between a necessary mental grasp of things and inner conversion, will be reflected throughout these pages.

Protecting Inner Vision

The Catholic imagination has to do with the revealing of the divine imagination as expressed first in creation, then in incarnation. And after that, in the *Now*.

> God's imagination is waiting to be discovered, hiding everywhere and in everyone. True catechesis is about revealing this extravagant omni-presence of God.

We need imagination to grasp that revelation.

Children have this imagination in abundance. Fresh from God, they still retain a sensitivity to the 'heaven that lies about them in their infancy', as Wordsworth puts it. Too soon it fades away, too soon it is taken from them – often by heart-less, head-centred programmes and preaching. Children need to be protected from our distortion of their innate, original intimacy with God. Once we forget how a mother devotedly loves her baby into a unique child, as teachers and preachers we will forever struggle to touch the hearts of those we serve with the fire of God's compassion.

> The holy task of the educator is not so much to fill their heads with new information, thus neglecting their original wholeness, but rather to lead them, as the mother does the baby, to the edge of their own divine possibilities.

Psychologist and author Alice Miller has written about 'the betrayal of children', that moment when a student's 'original spirituality and innate sense of lovableness' is damaged, or maybe destroyed forever. Is there a danger that in our silent complicity with not-so-subtle punishment/reward systems for academic performance, and in our forgetfulness of the real and holy needs in the souls of our students, that we, catechists, teachers and priests, rob or deny them of a wisdom and joy that is theirs by right?

The imagination of children, we have already pointed out, is made in the image of the divine imagination. Is part of our work, then, to protect the creativity and wildness in the imagination of children? How do we help adult enquirers to become aware of the divine beauty within them? Do we see catechesis as the work of recognising the signature of God written into the earth itself; of interpreting what is happening to us, of clarifying the hidden meaning of the daily lives we live and the relationships we are continually experiencing? How do we sharpen the focus for others to glimpse the divine imagination in all the stunning detail of a million species and a million human faces; to understand and believe that God loves difference? And what is the life-long effect on those around us if our attempts serve only to curb their unique creativity? Equally tragic, how blighted do our own lives become when we fail to honour the presence and promise of the *imago Dei* in our students?

The teacher sets them free to be faithful to their own original creativity. But by predetermining outcomes, by selecting only measurable, examinable content, we often set false limits for those we serve. Controlling systems, seeking a crippling conformity, erode the student's individuality and rob it of its true shape. In projecting our own fear of the free and unpredictable imagination, we often stunt the holy imagination in others. The divine never sets limits; but bad religious teaching does. The imagination does not come with a handbook of instructions; it is always free. It will never be amenable to systems of assessment. The spontaneous Spirit of the God of surprises is equally at home in the awkward, the wayward, the different, in those who march through the classrooms of their education, tuned-in to a different ipod.

How do we explain to children and adults that the warmth and excitement in their soul, its hope and delight, can only be from the God of mystery, creativity and artistry? Without a recovery of the idea of the divine imagination we will surely struggle. Nature and humanity are its mirrors. The study of God is the study of life in the light of the incarnation. The door to the human heart is the way to the inner heaven. Every human experience is a threshold to God.

How do we enable pupils, students, young and old, to protect their essential power to wonder and to imagine, and to know that these are the graces by which we are recognised as children of God? How do we set them free to dance the dance within them all, to sing the song of their souls, to listen to the whispers of their own hearts?

Anthony de Mello tells a story about the writer who came to interview the Master. 'People say you are a genius. Are you?' he asked. 'You might say so,' said the Master, none too modestly. 'And what makes one a genius?' 'The ability to recognise a butterfly in a caterpillar; an eagle in an egg; the saint in a selfish human being, the friend in the enemy.'

The gifted teacher knows that imagination is the cradle of possibility. She can discern the grace within those who may fail the expectations of the institution. She knows how to wait, how to look below the surface. And, we might add, to recognise the gifted child or adult in the unwilling or unpromising pupil.

How do we convince people that they are as free as they want to be; that they must refuse to accept whatever is shrinking their souls; making a prison out of their minds? How do we help people to identify the cages that surround them; the places in their hearts where they are still held bound and blindfold? To think imaginatively is to transcend all things negative; to transform the world, to liberate the divine. How do we dance out the dampness from our spirit and enter the spaces of the soul, of the mind, of the imagination, of the many rooms in the heaven within?

To think imaginatively is to liberate the divine.

By allowing ourselves to live in an enchanted, en-souled world and by sensing a deep significance in things everywhere, we live at a different, more satisfying depth. Normally we tend only to see the hard surfaces of things with a cold rationality. But once we grant interiority and intimacy to the world itself, then enchantment begins to stir. A postmodern world wants to explain everything in materialistic terms. It is slow to honour a 'presiding presence' in the world around us.

In *The Re-Enchantment of Everyday Life*, Thomas Moore writes, 'Appreciating the numinous, we don't accept any reductionistic explanations for human experience or the workings of the natural world. Nothing is stripped of its inherent spirituality, because, as theologians around the world have taught, divinity resides in all things. Every person, place, and object elicits reverence from us because of its essential numinosity – even the dilapidated building, the empty lot, the criminal on death row. Enchantment is nothing more than spirituality deeply rooted in the earth.'[16]

Divining the hidden spring

We need new words and images for dealing with the truly profound mysteries that currently challenge individuals and society. Without an adequate and timely theology we are left with secularist language and categories of thinking that fail us as we try to deal with questions of ultimate concern and spiritual import. Surprisingly for some, it is only an imaginative theology of enchantment that keeps the mystery of life infinitely open in the face of a secularism whose disciplines and methods bear the hallmarks of a closed and finite system.

'A theology of daily life would open our eyes to a dimension solidly sealed off by modern secularism, and it would restore soul, because soul is fed by the eternal and the spiritual as much as it finds nourishment in the temporal and the physical. Our universities and political institutions could begin to take theology seriously, placing it in the middle of the village rather than on the fringe, releasing it from its imprisonment in sectarianism, granting long-withheld life to our society which confesses its hunger for the spirit and its longing for the soul.'[17]

Because of the sacramental nature of their work, and the divine imagination they are called to work with, our educators – parish catechists, school teachers, parents, priests and governors – all may be regarded as alchemists of transformation, ministers who realise that their role lies in the persuading into the light what is already God-given, but hiding, within each student. This understanding leads to a radical shift in how we see our various pastoral educational roles. By way of preparation for the RCIA sessions, for instance, instead of filling her head with more knowledge to off-load on to passively-waiting recipients, the catechist will now try to empty herself of what she already knows so as to be in better shape for sharing with others, to be filled with their rich experiences.

> Her role and work now is about facilitating the opening of each heart to reveal its own mystery, with confidence, in the company of other soul-friends. For this to happen we need the sensitivity of the water-diviner, who walks over the fields with his quivering twig, in search of the hidden springs that wait beneath the surface.

Maybe the syllabuses we use are not appropriate for such an approach to teaching and learning, for the language and imagery of OTWTL, for the transmission of our Christian story in our multicultural parishes and schools. How to encompass the essential freedom of the Spirit as portrayed in the Catholic imagination within the parameters of the schemes and curricula that we are familiar with, is not always obvious. An excessive preoccupation with the totally cerebral 'handing on' of knowledge does not do justice to the rich vision of the incarnation.

The wild spirit of Jesus' teaching about the infinite wonder of the world, and the responsibilities and possibilities of each human heart, can never be relegated to the margins of our pastoral education. Maybe our beliefs and doctrines are too certain, too closed. Imagination and certainty are incompatible; imagination and possibility are twins. A premature certainty is the original sin of religion (and science!). 'It seems to me,' said Isaac Newton, 'that I'm like a child playing on the beach while the vast ocean of life lies unexplored around me.'

Imagination and certainty are incompatible; imagination and possibility are twins.

Above all, for those who are privileged to participate in exploring, with others, the Gracious Mystery we call God, such humility is becoming. It is the only way to stand before the vision of our faith as expressed in a theology of nature and grace, that has the power and inspiration to bring a freshness and vibrancy to the work of all educators of children

RESTORING THE SACRAMENTAL VISION   37

and adults in schools and parishes. But without the teacher's own inner transformation through contemplating the wonder of her calling, nothing much will ever happen. John Paul II insisted that only those 'who had fallen in love with God' would ever make a difference

Summary

The work of the artist (and the catechist) is to reveal what is hidden all around us.

As with the apostles after the resurrection, something prevents us from recognising the presence of Christ everywhere and in everyone.

The human is the threshold to the incarnate reality of God.

Bernano's country priest was seized by the Catholic imagination when he announced, in the face of enormous suffering and disappointment 'Grace is everywhere.' People need catechists, teachers and preachers to bring that hidden presence to light.

The experience of union with God is the ultimate goal of the curriculum.

Teachers, like parents, are co-creators, with God, of the kingdom.

The study of God is the study of life in the light of the incarnation.

A radical shift is needed in how we see our various pastoral educational roles.

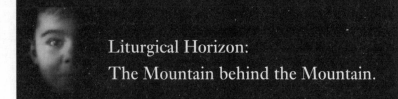

Liturgical Horizon:
The Mountain behind the Mountain.

This final section in Part One is an attempt to apply the transforming principle of the Catholic imagination to liturgy. There is a catechetical dimension to liturgical celebration that is powerfully revelatory. After further stories and reflections about sacramental vision, this section explores a way of looking at Eucharist, and at all liturgical moments, from a life-enhancing perspective. Ever faithful to the meaning of incarnation, a major role of liturgy is to gather up, name, purify, intensify and celebrate every dimension of what we call ordinary, daily life in its personal and universal dimensions. The role of all catechesis, teaching and preaching is the same.

One of the main purposes of this chapter is to suggest, again, that a true picture of the individual sacraments can only be authentically understood against the wider horizon of the rich notion of sacramentality. So much of the catechist's time is spent in sacramental catechesis and sacramental preparation for young and old. But so often we begin our teaching and explaining by offering the details of each sacrament without setting them in the broader context. The same principal holds true whether the topic or theme is the church, the world, or Jesus himself. Without the fundamental grasp of that traditional truth about the nature of sacrament, our faith will never really come alive in any deeply transforming way for ourselves or for others, in a world of deeply complex cultures. This is the Catholic perspective so central to the argument of OTWTL.

> There is an imaginative tradition and a long-established narrative infrastructure that, once it is recovered and clarified, may have much to say to those involved in Christian education in a modern milieu.

Even though this Catholic sensibility is still sadly neglected, it won't die out easily according to priest and story-teller John Shea and priest-sociologist Andrew Greeley. They believe that as long as Catholics tell stories (and most of them do not set out to tell stories, their narratives residing more in who they are, and what they do, rather than in what they say) then, the imagination will keep the vision alive.

The stories are told in the way the tellers absorb into their lives the ordinary and extraordinary events of life such as failure, disappointment, injustice, death, love, pleasure, marriage and birth. Such people 'reflect an enchantment that permeates the Catholic community, a haunting that hints powerfully at a salvation guaranteed by pervasive grace'.[18]

Dr Noel O'Donoghue writes of a Celtic sensitivity to the reality of worlds other than this one.

> 'The angelic world opens up at the margins of this world where a certain kind of imagination reveals tentatively and faintly, never obviously, a world of light so delicate and tenuous that it is blown away by both dogmatism and skepticism. It is a perception that needs to work through prayer, and that needs to be protected by a tradition of belief that must not harden into dogmatism.'

The poets of nature, such as Wordsworth and Hopkins, have made living contact with this tradition. Wordsworth looks behind the phenomena or 'appearances' of nature, and discovers within himself 'a sense of something deeply interfused' which has its dwelling 'in the light of setting suns and the round ocean and the living air'. Hopkins celebrates the unique 'inscape' of created things and makes the startling statement that when a human perceiver looks carefully and steadily at something in nature, the observed thing looks back at that person. So, too, T. S. Eliot finds in an urban wilderness the presence of 'an infinitely gentle, infinitely suffering thing'.[19] O'Donoghue quotes Kathleen Raine:

> I came too late to the hills. They were swept bare
> Winters before I was born of song and story,
> Of spell or speech with power of oracle or invocation ...
> A child I ran in the wind on a withered moor
> Crying out after those great presences who were not there,
> Long lost in the forgetfulness of the forgotten ...
> Yet I have glimpsed the bright mountain behind the mountain,
> Knowledge under the leaves, tasted the bitter berries red,
> Drunk cold water and clear from an inexhaustible fountain.[20]

Story and Imagination

One spring day Yehudi Menuhin was walking along a corridor in his Music Academy in Paris. He came across a young student tucking into his lunch. The maestro paused and enquired about the chunky bread that was quickly disappearing. The boy explained that his mother, who lived on the west coast of Ireland, had baked this particular blend of soda bread for her son. She had then carefully wrapped it up and posted the parcel of hearty nourishment to young Liam. The famous man was very touched by this story as he reflected on the love that this woman would have poured into the dough she was carefully kneading. She would have walked or cycled with it to the Post Office. It would then have crossed the seas to the beloved of her heart. Maybe the musician was remembering some lines from *The Prophet*: 'Work is love made visible ... if you bake bread with indifference you make a bitter bread that feeds but half man's hunger.'[21]

There is something of the sacramental imagination in this story. It is a very ordinary account of an everyday moment. But it reveals the love hidden behind the simple act, the bread behind the bread, the story behind the story. Like art, poetry and music, the sacramental imagination preserves and expresses the hidden closeness and distance of things, it hints and guesses at the divine potential of things. Without a vibrant sense of sacramentality the enchantment of Christianity will be lost, the immanent and transcendent will drift away from each other, and, as W. B. Yeats reminded us, all evidence of God will be erased from the earth. Without imaginative story only dead doctrine remains.

Without imaginative story only dead doctrine remains.

In *Meditations from a Moving Chair*, Andre Dubus reveals an acute sense of sacramentality. 'A sacrament is physical and within it is God's love; as a sandwich is physical, and nutritious, and pleasurable, and within it is love, if someone makes it for you and gives it to you with love; even harried or tired or impatient love, but with love's direction and concern, love's again and again wavering and distorted focus on goodness, then God's love too is in the sandwich.' Andrew Greeley comments that the sandwich becomes enchanted because it is permeated by, dense in, awash with the two loves – human and divine.[22]

The Catholic imagination, or, according to David Tracy, the analogical imagination, in all its many manifestations, emphasises the metaphorical nature of creation. 'The objects, events, and persons of ordinary existence hint at the nature of God and indeed make God present to us. Everything in creation, from the exploding cosmos to the whirling, dancing, and utterly mysterious quantum particles, discloses something about God and, in so doing, brings God among us. The love of God for us, in perhaps the boldest of all metaphors (and one with which the church has been perennially uneasy) is like the passionate love between man and woman. God lurks in physical human love and reveals himself to us (to the two humans themselves first of all) through it. Eventually the church came to see that human love was indeed a sacrament which discloses God's grace and makes it present among us.'[23]

To summarise briefly, it will be difficult for our teachers and catechists to do justice to the wonder of the incarnation without a sure sense of the reality of the sacramental vision, and of how it can be interiorised only through the uses of the imagination, and how the whole mystery of it is grounded in a theology of nature and grace.

How do you enable students to perceive the presence of God in every aspect of their own lives, in the human condition as a whole, and in all creation? How is that Catholic imagination set free to view the world and all that is in it, as enchanted, haunted by the Holy Spirit and enveloped in grace? Once we forget the fundamental truth of the indwelling Spirit of God, we will ever communicate only flat facts. Where there is no vision there is no transformation. Without the memory of the mystery, the heart will never be engaged. The work of the teacher and catechist is to awaken others to what they already are – the body of Christ. 'I cannot imagine what else a teacher or preacher should do,' wrote Leon Tolstoy, 'except to remind people of their capacity for the infinite.'

It is difficult to overstate the importance of preserving a sacramental vision in the handing on of the faith. This vision is the gift of Jesus. It enables us to see into, and beyond things, in the light of God's love. We are redeemed by our total belonging to Christ who was (and is) this vision. He was the first to reveal the true meaning at the heart of the works of his Father. He himself was the 'walking sacrament' of God's infinite compassion. His body was the primordial and most real symbol of the essential truth of the world and of our lives. In him we see the love and meaning at the heart of everything. That is the sacramental vision. In that truth lies our salvation. That is the prized gift that we do all in our power to hand over accurately to each generation, and in all parts of the world. Without our grace-filled imagination there will be no vibrant heartbeat of God heard in the world. Only spiritless, alienating religion.

Jesus was the 'walking sacrament' of God's infinite compassion.

This sacramental insight, though lost to mainstream preaching and teaching, has not died out completely. It is a hardy survivor in the Catholic world. But for how long more? Andrew Greeley remembers that it was nurtured in young hearts by story, feast-days, home-made ritual, processions and prayers. It has not disappeared from our faith, he claims; it has only gone to sleep. And it is high time for a new awakening.[24]

Sacramental Poetics – and its cost

'A sacramental poetics is about transformation, the transforming of everyday perception and experience into something that satisfies the deepest longings. A sacramental poetics appeals to the imagination; by appealing to the basic realities in our lives – bread, water, oil, salt, earth, trees, in word and symbol, prayer and gesture – it awakens a depth dimension and an experience of the sacred. Sacramental poetics has the potential to re-enchant a broken-hearted world, speaking the language and the music of the heart to the addicted consumer, the jaded, hypnotised slave of the market.'[25]

Professor Mary Grey rues the lack of the appreciation of beauty and of sacramental poetics in the life of faith. Music, poetry, art and architecture nourish the soul and prepare the ground for essential transformation. Each night and day, in the unfolding of our universe, and of our lives in community, is teeming with sacramental moments.

> Those human, spiritual moments are poured out from the heart of the Gracious Mystery in the daily realities and the ordinary experiences of our lives. They are largely ignored in the church's official definitions of sacraments and in the syllabuses of our schools and catechetical guidelines of our parishes.

They are often ignored, too, Greeley holds, referring to the North American church practice, in 'what passes for liturgy in many parishes. If the liturgical imagination continues to survive, it will do so despite the "liturgists" and not because of them. Its strength is rooted in the depths of the Catholic psyche with its ability to sense grace lurking everywhere.'[26] Is it asking too much of our faithful pastoral ministers to reflect deeply within themselves about the ways and means of keeping that vision alive in their own hearts first, and then of connecting with that same potential in others?

We are all blessed with mystical potential as well as with a more practical one; with a contemplative mind as well as a more calculating one; with a readiness for break-through into true wisdom as well as with growth in knowledge and facts; with a potential for real transformation as well as with increased understanding. Jesus was forever calling us forward into our true humanity and away from our fallen condition. He was always removing the suffocating boundaries of fear that we place around ourselves, and revealing the infinite horizons in accord with our divine destiny. Now grace may be gift; it does not follow that it is always easy.

In our super-charged, over-stressed lives, how does the teacher or parish minister find time for timeless things – for the watching and waiting that are the necessary prerequisites for sacramental vision, for developing a mystical presence, for a painful growing into a sense of the sacred? When OTWTL unfolds its theology of nature and grace, what is also implied for those who hope to ingest and live and work out of that theology, is a lot of dying and rising, of splintering and mending, in the process of transformation.

'Are you prepared to break your heart and mind,' Archbishop Rowan Williams asks, 'to purify and clarify your vision?' Is it fair to invite our educators into this new way of being and seeing? Have they not enough on their plates already? And are they not doing a very good job as it is? And yet, it cannot be denied, that there is a huge interest, readiness and openness in our catechists and teachers to be filled with deep conviction, to be fired up with a new vision, to be led to another place of perception, in the graced work they do.

'Are you prepared to break your heart and mind,' Archbishop Rowan Williams asks, 'to purify and clarify your vision?'

The contemplative vision springs from the loving observation of what is. 'Tenderness comes from long looking' wrote Theodore Roethke. What Mary Grey calls 'sacramental perception' comes only after disciplined focusing. But when it does we are captivated for life. It is about a quality of presence, about what scientist-writer Annie Dillard describes as truly 'being there':

> 'I saw the backyard cedar where the mourning doves roost, charged and transfigured, each cell buzzing with flame. I stood on the grass with lights in it, grass that was wholly fire, utterly focused and utterly dreamed. It was less like seeing than like being seen for the first time, knocked breathless by a powerful glance. The flood of fire abated, but I'm still spending the power ... The vision comes and goes, mostly goes, but I live for it, for the moment when the mountains open and a new light roars in spate through the crack, and the mountains slam.'[27]

We can sense the same intensity when Dillard writes about the Mass. She warns about our casual, routine approach to the highest moment of worship. Through banal, unimaginative repetition have we trivialised the unique and wild eucharistic power and presence? All kinds of worlds collide, and the deepest forces of light and darkness are drawn into war and play at the table of sacrifice.

Dillard writes about the need to 'fasten our seat-belts and wear crash-helmets' in church on Sunday morning because of the shocking, dangerous and life-long impact of the Mass on our personal lives and on the development of the universe.

'The sleeping God may wake up', she warns, 'and reveal the TNT that we're playing around with!' What we're 'playing around' with is the deadly serious game of transforming the world, its death and darkness, its greed and nihilism, its evil and pain into the body of God. 'This is the way the world is, altar and cup.' It is about drawing out, from within the mysterious chaos of ourselves and the cosmos, the divine image. It is about preparing for that day 'in the new world' when, in peace and equality, in fairness and justice, the Host of Heaven will 'gather people of every race, language and way of life, to share in the one eternal banquet' for ever and ever. (Eucharistic Prayer II for Reconciliation)

The Liturgy of Life

'The theology of grace that informs Vatican II recovers "the ordinary" as the realm of grace, God's better beauty; hence the aesthetic of holiness is not something exceptional but something that is shaped in the realm of the domestic, giving to it the weight of glory; the alchemist's stone is Christ.

> The liturgy is the routine inscription of eternity in time, the continual action of Christ who is Lord of time, and the Spirit that moves over the dark aporetic abyss of history to bring forth Life. In the liturgy the 'ordinary' is consecrated and made the place of encounter ...

By its very 'routine' and 'ordinariness' the liturgy writes us into time; in its rhythms and seasons, it celebrates our finitude and our embodiedness. It is not an escape from the trials and contradictions of our finite temporal existence to eternity, but a way of seeing them within the greater horizon of God's eternal life and the continual action of his Love.'[28]

The liturgy of the world and the liturgy of the church.

It is useful to speak of two liturgies – the liturgy of the world and liturgy of the church; the sacrament of the universe and the sacrament of the Mass; the table of our lives and the table of the bread and wine. We need to celebrate the one as we celebrate the other. If we are not in a holy communion with the God of Life in the routine lives we live, we will hardly experience a great intimacy at the Holy Communion of Mass.

Rahner reminds us that the Christian 'receives under holy signs the true Body of the Lord, knowing this to be worthless, were he not to communicate with that Body of God which is the world itself and its fate; he partakes of the one Body so as to remain in communion with that other body which is the reality of his life.'[29]

The first aim in an authentic liturgical catechesis is, as we have been emphasising, to present sacramentality and the sacraments as of a piece with our lives in our world; to see them in the context of a world already permeated with God's presence, encompassed by divine love. In the very person of Christ himself, this intimate unity has taken place. The human is now the address of the divine, the raw material of our redemption. 'Salvation' wrote Tertullian, 'hinges on the flesh.' The art is to enable this revelation to be known, gladly accepted, and celebrated; to enable people to accept 'who they already are'.

To the analytical mind sacramental grace may seem to be a complicated phenomenon which needs many terms and treatises; to the mystic it is a simple, rich and enriching experience bringing the kind of knowing that surpasses all knowledge. To the calculating mind the notion of the sacramental imagination is too undefined and risky, too vague to measure, too unreachable to possess; to the contemplative mind it is the beckoning horizon of love and meaning that transforms the soul and enlightens the wavering heart. There is a paradigm of rubrical uniformity; and there is a paradigm of life-giving worship.

Vatican II's *The Church in the Modern World* makes it clear that in the past we over-emphasised the notion of two distinct worlds – one profane, the other sacred. Gregory Baum, a peritus at the Council, explains:

> 'The radical distinction between sacred and profane, between
> nature and grace, has been overcome in the person of Christ. In
> Christ it is revealed that the locus of the divine is the human. In
> him it made manifest that God speaks in and through the words
> and gestures of people.

Christian liturgy, therefore, can no longer consist in sacred rites by which people are severed from the ordinary circumstance of their lives. The liturgy, rather, is the celebration of the deepest dimension of human life, which is God's self-communication to all humanity. Liturgy unites people more closely to their daily lives. Worship remembers and celebrates the marvellous things God works in the lives of human beings, purifies and intensifies these gifts, makes everyone more sensitive to the Word and Spirit present in their daily lives.'[30]

It is vital for pastoral ministers, if their educational work is to bear lasting and transforming fruit, and if they believe that grace reveals the true essence of nature, to be true to this insight in the way they catechise and explain the connection between liturgy and life. If the presence of the Creator is not sensed in the ordinary events of each day, then the odds are that God will not be sensed in sacramental celebration either. If we find no hint of divine immanence in the emotions and experiences of our lives, then, it is highly unlikely that we will touch the closeness of God at the liturgical assembly.

The creative teacher or catechist will realise that, in one sense, the whole world is her oyster when it comes to selecting 'content' for her educational work. Once she is deeply familiar with the revealed story of creation and incarnation, then all kinds of things – the beauty, goodness or pain of a particular experience, for instance – can be a compelling disclosure of the presence of God. When someone, say, has had a celebration with friends, a birth, accident or tragedy in the family, a new experience or great surprise – all of these can be powerful experiences of absolute mystery. The catechist or liturgist will be urging the students to be increasingly attentive to the hidden secrets in the present moment, to 'the music of what happens', in the ambiguous and challenging circumstances of a life that seems seriously out of tune.

BE attentive to the hidden secrets in the present moment.

When the liturgy is celebrated with this understanding in mind, heart and body, a deep change will then take place. The profound relevance of redemptive grace to each person's condition will inspire hearts with a new urgency for a deeper kind of loving and living. This heightened awareness is a huge step in claiming and living the promised, abundant life.

Shortly after his inauguration, Pope Benedict called for a greater sense of beauty in liturgy so as to achieve this awareness. 'If the church is to continue to transform and to humanise the world, how can she dispense with beauty in her liturgies, that beauty which is so closely linked with love, and with the radiance of the Resurrection?'

The Eucharistic Prism

Throughout OTWTL there are seeds of a wonderfully all-embracing vision of the meaning of liturgy, sacraments and Eucharist. Once we accept the place of imagination and of sacramental perception into our understanding of the Eucharist, for instance, then a whole new horizon of comprehension moves in front of us. After the incarnation itself, the Eucharist is the richest expression of the love and meaning at the heart of creation and within our own graced lives. And this expression has to be symbolic, encapsulated in time and space.

How can catechists and teachers find a simple but profound strategy for bringing the Mass to life? How do they reveal new depths to its mystery? A deeper understanding is reached when what is done around the altar is connected with what happens each day of our life. Eucharist is celebrated so as to make present for us today, the once-for-all Blessed Night of the incarnation, and to never forget its implications for our ordinary routines and chores. The Mass can be understood as the 'colouring in' of the pale outlines of grace in the fallen lives we bring to it; as revealing the true worth of all that is going on within us and around us – disclosing and celebrating the hidden presence of God in the midst of the most common and even sinful things.

It could be said that the separate, often discordant notes of each day's living are fused into one flowing Sunday symphony; that the hurts, fears and shame of our lives are all held and embraced in this weekly ritual of bread and wine; that the Eucharist creates stories and poems out of the mixed-up alphabet of what happens each day.

> The Eucharist guarantees that everything in our life is sacred; that nothing is lost; that no bitter tear or heartfelt wish is ever wasted; that nothing is 'merely' human any more; that no sin is ever left unredeemed; that everything, in the end, is harvest.

Pastoral educators need to be helped to transcend an over-emphasis on the rubrics and the liturgical niceties of the daily or weekly ritual. Life is incredibly raw and violent. Passions ignite in a moment. Fierce emotions wage silent civil wars in the hidden places of our hearts. This is the raw material of the Sunday Mass. If it is not about our volatile, erratic and incredibly powerful drives and emotions, then the Word has become flesh in vain. Where else can redemption happen if not at the point of pain? From what else, other than the ever-present fear, jealousy, anger and despair, can people be saved? If the hard-won Eucharist of the Passover is to have any relevance to our lives, it must be felt at the very guts and marrow of our being, at those precarious places within us where our demons and angels meet. This is where our need is strong and most urgent.

We must transcend an over-emphasis on rubrics.

John Paul II describes this need of God's healing in the Eucharist 'as physical as the need for food or water'. He said that our desire for personal transformation is expressed in wanting an intimacy with God which is 'instinctive and physical'. 'It is not by chance,' he says, 'that the psalmist speaks of an embrace, of a clinging that is almost physical.'

Before he died, having exhausted what he could do with words, Jesus went beyond them. He gave us the Eucharist, his physical presence, his kiss, a ritual within which he holds us to his heart. Touch, not words, is what we often need. God has to pick us up, like a mother her child. Skin needs to be touched, Richard Rohr reminds us. Our bodies have their senses to be nourished. There are times when even holy words are not enough. Incarnation becomes necessary to assuage our ache for love.

As well as being a kind of prism that draws out the true colours of daily, personal life in community, the Eucharist is also a cosmic prism that reflects God's colours in the wider universe. The Catholic sacramental imagination understands and rejoices when, with bread and wine, the whole universe is seen to be acknowledging its very being as flowing from the womb of God from the beginning of time and through each passing moment. Around the table bearing the fruits of the earth and the work of human hands, through the human voices, gesture and ritual of its children, the very cosmos itself is in worship before its Creator, offering itself to its incomprehensible lover-God in the ecstasy of its joys and the bitterness of its sorrows.

The very cosmos itself is in worship before its Creator.

In his Jubilee letter *Tertio Millennio Adveniente* Pope John Paul II reveals his intimations of the cosmic nuances of entering the third Millennium. He writes out of a theology of nature and grace. 'The fact that in the fullness of time the Eternal Word took on the condition of a creature, gives a unique cosmic value to the event which took place in Bethlehem two thousand years ago. Thanks to the Word, the world of creatures appears as a cosmos, an ordered universe. And it is the same Word, who by taking flesh, renews the cosmic order of creation.'

In her reflections on the Eucharistic transformation of ourselves and of the cosmos, Mary Grey quotes Etty Hillesum's last entry in her diary before being transported to her death in Auschwitz: 'All I want to say is this: the misery here is quite terrible, and yet, late at night when the day has slunk away into the deaths behind me, I often walk with a spring in my step along the barbed wire. And then, time and again, it soars straight from my heart – I can't help it, that's just the way it is, like some elementary force – the feeling that life is glorious and magnificent, and that one day we shall be building a whole new world.'[31] For mystics and martyrs, this is a Eucharistic moment.

A Catholic imagination weaves wonderful colours into the textures of all the sacraments. There is a sacramental vision that draws undreamt-of and heart-warming dimensions from each of the seven sacraments. Every sacrament is paradigmatic of the sacramentality of each human heart and of all creation.

'We live in our bodies; our spirituality is corporeal. Our redemption lies in the real world of space and time, the only world in which we can live. It is here, and nowhere else, that God's great work is accomplished.'[32] A theology of nature and grace provides the much-needed horizon and context within which we hold this truth and within which we situate all our teaching and preaching. It is the traditional catalyst that guarantees the connectedness of all things – that, in the end, in the world of God, everything belongs.

Summary

Without imaginative story only dead doctrine remains; before dogma began there was only story.

Where there is no vision there is no transformation.

The work of the catechist is to awaken others to what they already are – the body of Christ.

Jesus was the walking sacrament of God's compassion.

Music, poetry, art and architecture nourish the soul and provide a window to God's beauty.

There are not two distinct worlds – one secular, one sacred.

At the Eucharist we celebrate the hidden presence of God in all our experiences, in all creation.

In the liturgy of the church we name, express and celebrate in visible and tangible form, the fundamental grace that lies hidden in the world – in the routine of daily living, in all human experience, in the totality of creation. Ours is an embodied Christianity

Courageous Conversations

Put yourself in courageous conversation with the cliff-edge of your life, no matter how frightening it seems. Courageous conversation needs courageous hearts. *(David Whyte)*

What would you describe as 'peak experiences' in your life? In what way would you connect them with God's presence? Can you remember those lasting moments when you were transformed, those places of grace when your faith became an experience? What special moments or peak-moments will never leave you?

From where, for you, is God absent? Can we speak of naming grace in human experience in the face of radical suffering? Can limited and sinful human beings, and divided human communities, enflesh and proclaim the incarnate presence of God in the world? In the midst of ecological devastation can we announce that God is revealed throughout creation?

When have your ordinary experiences found expression in the Sunday liturgy? At a wedding? A baptism? A funeral? First Communion? A personal experience? Where do you feel the presence of God most – at

Mass or in your ordinary life? Is there a connection between both kinds of awareness? Does your religious practice validate or negate the truth of your common experiences? How would you describe the connection between the 'liturgy of life' and the 'liturgy of the church'; between daily living and celebrating the Eucharist?

What part does imagination play in the way you believe? How would you describe the relationship between imagination and faith? Do you rate highly the role of 'story' in the work you do?

Are we witnessing the beginning of a timely theological renewal, the building of a deeper base for prophetic commitment to the urgent issues of justice, freedom and peace? How do we ensure that 'the sacramental vision' will engage with the crisis of communication – of transmission and relevance – probably the greatest current challenge for a multi-cultural, post-modern Catholic inner-city parish or school today? What part might parents, teachers, priests and catechists play in the critical engagement between the church and a contemporary culture of shifting meaning?

Part Two

Welcoming Theology

There is a joy about studying and 'doing' theology. It is a creative and fulfilling kind of work. Understanding things is so satisfying. We are creatures forever seeking a deeper comprehension of the mystery of ourselves and of God. The study of theology needs to be set free. Even though the academic study of theology is now engaged in by an increasing number of lay people, it still exists, in a pastoral sense, on the sidelines of our faith. Perhaps this is the time when it can be restored to centre stage again. All evangelising, catechising, teaching and preaching is based on a theology. It is important that we should be able to articulate it. Otherwise we do not have a ground to stand or build on. The Vatican II theology outlined in OTWTL is both imaginative and sacramental. It offers a vision of creation and incarnation that brings a new dynamism to our own faith and therefore, to our ministry in the classroom and the parish-room.

God is the ultimate and absolute source of all being; but this universal principle of creation – the *Logos*, primordial reason – is at the same time a lover with all the passion of a true love. *Eros* is thus supremely ennobled, yet at the same time it is so purified as to become one with *agape* ... we experience the love of God, we perceive his presence and we learn to recognise that presence in our daily lives.

Benedict XVI

As disciples we find God in and through our humanity. In a very real sense there is nowhere where God is not. Given that human beings are created in God's image, the pinnacle of creation, and the fact that God chose to become a human person, it is possible to see the mystery of God in the mystery of our humanity.

Archbishop Vincent Nichols

Theology cannot be expressed solely in the sleek and passionless form of the treatise, but demands movement, sharp debate ... the virile conversation of deep and powerful emotion.

Hans Urs von Balthasar

The breakdown of classical culture ... and the manifest comprehensiveness of modern culture confront Catholic philosophy and Catholic theology with the gravest of problems, imposing upon them mountainous tasks, inviting them to Herculean labours.

Bernard Lonergan

The religious educator is at once theologian and educator, for the field of religious education is located at the point where theology and education meet.

Richard McBrien

Theology of Humanity:
A Ground to Stand On

On the Way to Life urges us to reconsider the still untapped potential of the Second Vatican Council, especially the promise that lies within a rediscovery of what it calls the Catholic imagination and the sacramental vision. There is a theology of nature and grace that sees Revelation as the amazing love-story of God's desire to be intimately among us in human form. Full of compassion, God wished to create the world out of pure love, and then, in time, to become that creation. That 'becoming' happened in Jesus Christ. In OTWTL we read about the re-emergence of a rich understanding of human nature grounded in grace. What makes us truly human is the instinct for God that we all carry – an instinct that is already God's gift to us in creation, and revealed to be so in the incarnation. The intimate at-one-ness between God and creation is established, once and forever, in the person of Christ. Dualism is everything that separates God's own creation and God's own people from God's own self. All dualism ended the night that God was born into our world in the shape of the infant Jesus.

Revelation is the self-communication of God. This divine self-disclosing always happens sacramentally. According to a theology of nature and grace, the revelation within incarnation is best understood in terms of our awakening to the profound reality of being human, since humanity and all of creation is God's way of being present in the world. Revelation is about the unlimited possibilities of humanity, graced at its centre from the very beginning. It is about God's desire to be known and loved in Jesus Christ, the Human One, and in the integrity of all creation. We can say, with saints and theologians from the time of Christ, that the incarnation happened, not just because creation went wrong at some early stage, but because, in God's plan to share God's own divine joy with others, creation was first necessary so that incarnation could take place. The event of incarnation only explicates in the light what is already afoot and hidden within human existence from the first creation. 'What is chronologically first,' wrote Gabriel Moran, 'must be understood in the light of the later, full revelation.'

An impressive array of theological stars including Aquinas, Tillich, von Balthasar, Schillebeeckx and Rahner, while obviously differing on many fronts, have all held that it is not possible to speak theologically about God without at the same time saying something about humanity, and vice versa. A theology centred on humanity is not in opposition to a theology centred on Christ. Christian anthropology only attains its full meaning when it conceives of the human being as the openness and capacity for union with God. Nor are any of these theologians under any illusion about the utter devastation caused by the reality of original sin at the heart of creation, and consequently, about humanity's need of redemption.

A theology centred on humanity is not in opposition to a theology centred on Christ.

Vatican I and II remind us that, when God was creating Adam, it was the human form of the Son, the ever-present Word, the divine self incarnate, that was uppermost in God's mind. In the *Divine Office*, we read: 'In his own image God created man, and when from dust he fashioned Adam's face, the likeness of his only Son was formed; his Word incarnate, filled with truth and grace.' Adam was the long-term preparation for Jesus – a sort of proto-type of him who was to come. 'There is no difficulty,' Rahner assures us, 'in thinking that the first, primal and comprehensively eternal will of God is his own self-expression and that in this act of will, God wills the humanity of Christ, and hence all humanity and creation in general, as its setting ... God's creative act always drafts the creature as the paradigm of a possible utterance of himself.'[1]

St Paul preaches that all of us are 'copies of the glorious body of Christ'. St Leo the Great wrote: 'O Christian heart, recognise the great worth of the wisdom that is yours, so that the creator may be shown forth in the creature and that, in the mirror of your heart as in the lines of a portrait, the image of God may be reflected.' As Richard McBrien points out: 'Every human person is already radically open to divine revelation in the very core of his or her being, in that God is present to every person as an offer of grace'.[2]

Reclaiming the Human

The authors of OTWTL understand divine grace and human nature as inextricably linked. This fundamental connection is their basis for the reclaiming of a unique Christian understanding of humanity – a Christological humanism. Creation is already held and fashioned in grace because it is, so to speak, the rough-draft of the shape of God.

> A truly incarnational theology is based on the simple, but profound fact that, as Rahner says, 'what we call sanctifying grace and divine life is present everywhere –wherever, in fact, man (*sic*) does not close himself to the God of salvation.

For we know that this grace is being communicated, even though in ways that are partially anonymous and hidden, within the concrete reality and history of human life.'[3]

In a sacramental model, the authors of OTWTL tell us, grace is seen as intrinsic to human nature. 'Extrinsicism' (where grace is not inherent), they write, 'tended to reinforce a dualistic way of thinking that sees nature and super-nature in an uneasy complementarity at best, and an oppositional dualism, at worst.' We cannot think of human nature independently of grace. Moreover, 'if grace is integral to nature, then all nature in some way has the capacity to disclose grace and be a vehicle for it'.[4] We can hold that nature itself is intrinsically graced from the start.

Nature itself is intrinsically graced.

Another way of looking at this fascinating mystery is to consider the notion of 'humanism' endorsed by OTWTL. A Christological humanism is always seeking to understand the human as the *imago Dei*, the image of God. The authors explain that 'the Council (Vatican II) develops a powerful discourse on "the human" so as to engage with the "humanism" of modernity and use it as a meeting ground. The "human" is reclaimed as an explicitly Christian sphere ... The Council makes the church one of the most powerful defenders of "the human", the dignity and destiny of every person, irrespective of their birth, nationality, status or abilities.'[5]

The following very useful comment is made in OTWTL: Introductory Material: 'Vatican II proposes an understanding of humanity which accepts what contemporary culture has to say about it in part, but completes it with the rich vision of humanity and its history transformed in Christ, so that human beings and their culture may be seen as sacramental, finite realities which display the being of God because God has made his dwelling in them.' (p 13) This is part of the attraction of a theology of creation and incarnation. It lovingly treasures, respects and celebrates everything that is good and beautiful in the human condition. Then, in its Christian wisdom, it insists on the need for healing and completing, so as to bring all its holy promise to its fullness, in the light and likeness of God.

Without a theological ground to stand on, any renewal of the church's work during these times of many cultures will be but another temporary, limited and fragmented effort. The authors of OTWTL insist that we must have confidence in our theology of nature and grace. 'It is essentially a theology that makes explicit the "eternity in the heart" of every human person which is constantly seeking expression and form. The sacramental vision of Catholicism is the sacrament of the (human) heart as well, and cannot help but find a deep resonance there ... The theology of grace that informs Vatican II recovers "the ordinary" as the realm of grace, God's "better beauty"; hence the aesthetic of holiness is not something exceptional but something that is shaped in the realm of the domestic, giving to it the weight of glory; the alchemist's stone is Christ.'[6]

> Nothing is 'ordinary' or 'merely natural or human' anymore; in the light of incarnation all creation is revealed in its truest origin and deepest significance.

It is the mystical dimensions in our truly traditional theologies that set our spirits free to explore the mystery of God. 'All natural things were produced by the divine artist, and so may be called God's works of art,' wrote the Angelic Doctor Aquinas, 'Just as flaming comes up with fire, so the existence of any creature comes up with the divine presence.' There is something earthy and deeply satisfying in the sacramental vision of St Thomas. Regarding beauty and light he has much to say: 'God is beauty itself, beautifying all things with a holy beauty ... God puts into creatures, along with a kind of sheen, a reflection of God's own luminous ray, which is the fountain of all light. From this Beautiful One beauty comes to be in all beings.'

A Shift in Focus

The recovery of this neglected perspective requires a profound shift in focus for the average Catholic. Karl Rahner tries to explain how the secular world is, from the outset, always encompassed and infused with the grace of God's self-communication. 'The world is permeated by the grace of God ... Creation is constantly and ceaselessly possessed by grace from its innermost roots ... Whether the world knows it or not, this is so.'[7] Grace has been offered to the world from the very beginning of its existence, by virtue of the fact that it is created as a potential recipient of divinity. Grace is, therefore, available always and everywhere. This is the vision of the sacramental imagination. Without that gift, the teacher and preacher will be telling the wrong story.

While there are significant differences in the various emphases of von Balthasar and Rahner, the main thrust of their theology is forever weaving itself around the twin threads of the incarnational tapestry – the story of God's gracious self-communication to the individual, the community, the universe, on the one hand, and, on the other, the world's efforts to respond to this invitation. What is of supreme importance for the Christian to remember and believe is the fact that this eternal offer, this spoken word of love, has been perfectly heard and responded to, once for all and irrevocably, in the life of Jesus, in what the Council of Ephesus called 'the hypostatic union'.

> Christ completed and perfected what God began in creation by being at once 'the way forward' for the final irrevocable breakthrough of humanity into God and 'the way in' for the ever-approaching, self-disposing love of God for humanity.

His is the fullness of humanity that we all aspire to. We are not so much human beings trying to become spiritual, as spiritual beings trying to become truly human. Christ is not the super-human being; he is the norm, we the abnormal. He is the true, we are out of true. 'He does not reveal,' Fr Hugh Lavery wrote, 'what it is to be divine; he reveals what it is to be human. We are already spiritual; we become human.'[8]

Many such insights are sourced from Vatican II. *Gaudium et spes* makes clear that the locus of revelation is the living experience of humanity and its meaning in the light of Christ, the Human One. 'The truth is that only in the light of the incarnate Word does the mystery of man take on light. For Adam, the first man, was a figure of him who was to come, namely Christ the Lord. Christ the final Adam, by the revelation of the mystery of the Father and his love, fully reveals man to man himself, and makes his supreme calling clear ... He worked with human hands, he thought with a human mind, he acted by human choice, and he loved with a human heart.'[9] Rudolf Bultmann sums up this revealed truth succinctly: 'The light that appeared in Jesus is none other than that which had already shone forth in creation.' And none other, we may add, than that which shines forth in all of us today.

He worked with human hands, he thought with a human mind, he acted by human choice, and he loved with a human heart.

Is that light which shines forth from the heart of things an example of what OTWTL calls 'a surplus of meaning'? Thomas Aquinas wrote about the 'radiance' and 'overflow of presence' in created things.

Archbishop Rowan Williams, discussing beauty and modernism, writes about an 'overplus of significance' within all that exists. It is as though there is much more to everything than at first glance appears to be the case. The French philosopher Jacques Maritain used a celebrated phrase about 'things being more than they are'; they 'give more than they have'. We are certainly in the land of imagination and sacramentality here. And of humble silence, too. There is no other way to approach the untranslatable mystery of the first Word, yet a mystery that is forever seeking expression in the eternity of the human heart. All of these reflections are waiting to be offered again to a brilliant, confused world that has so much to offer to us, too, in turn.

'The visible, the tangible, the finite, the historical – all these are actual or potential carriers of the divine presence,' writes Richard McBrien, professor of theology at Notre Dame University, 'It is only in and through these material realities that we can encounter the invisible God ... Catholicism insists that the dichotomy between nature and grace is eliminated. Human existence is already graced existence. There is no merely natural end of human existence, with a supernatural end imposed from above. Human existence in its natural, historical condition is radically oriented toward God. This history of the world is, at the same time, the history of salvation'[10]

There is no dichotomy between nature and grace.

Edward Schillebeeckx argues that this has to be so. Without incarnation there could be no encounter between God and the human community. It is only in so far as God surrenders to our material condition that God can reach us and that we can reach God. This embodiment of the spiritual in the material is called the sacramental principle. Incarnational realism makes impossible the existence of 'pure nature'.

> Grace is not something added to, or superimposed upon, nature. Rather, nature is always constituted in, and oriented toward, the covenant between God and humanity in Christ.

Grace, therefore, supposes nature, and nature supposes grace. The human heart is *naturaliter religiosa*. This non-negotiable theological insight must always remain absolutely central in our approaches to the work of evangelising and educating.

In *Catholicism Confronts Modernity*, Langdon Gilkey holds that 'the love of life, the appreciation of the body in the senses, of joy and celebration, the tolerance of the sinner, these natural, worldly, and "human" virtues are far more clearly and universally embodied in Catholics and Catholic life than in Protestantism.' He goes on to add that this Catholic sacramental principle 'may provide the best entrance into a new synthesis of the Christian tradition with the vitalities as well as the relativities of contemporary existence.'[11]

John Paul II, himself no stranger to such a theology of creation and revelation, adds significantly to these soul-stirring insights in his *The Holy Spirit in the Life of the Church and of the World*: 'The incarnation of God the Son signifies the taking up into unity with God not only human nature, but in this human nature, in a sense, everything that is flesh ... the incarnation then, also has a cosmic significance, a cosmic dimension; the first-born of creation unites himself in some way with the entire reality of man, within the whole of creation.'[12]

The incarnation has a cosmic significance.

Later still, in *Ecclesia de Eucharistia*, in a supreme moment of pure sacramental imagination, the Pope wrote about his powerful experience of the universal and cosmic character of the Eucharist. 'Yes, cosmic!' he wrote, 'Because even when the Eucharist is celebrated on the humble altar of a country church, it is always, in some way, celebrated on the altar of the world. It unites heaven and earth. It embraces and permeates all creation.'[13] Are there not T. S. Eliot-like 'hints and guesses' already emerging here, for the evangelising work of the church, in these papal insights into the meaning of creation, incarnation, eucharist and our holy, broken humanity?

Living Theology

There is a great joy in exploring and 'doing' theology. Good, living theology provides a meaning, a context and a resonance for our educational work and our very being as Christians. One of the reasons for our difficulties with dogma and doctrines is their loss of relevance for our lives. Beliefs are not ends in themselves. They exist to bring us to a deeper understanding of the inexhaustible mystery that is God and God's involvement with us. Once theology or belief loses contact with experience, they become empty formulas with no personal meaning.

Dr Dermot Lane, former Director of Studies at Mater Dei Institute of Education in Dublin, reminds us that theology, from beginning to end, is about the critical unpacking of the revelation of God that takes place in human experience through faith. OTWTL invites us to do theology in a new key. *Begin with the Heart* is an attempt to provide a critical foundation for faith in the revelation of God by appealing to the richness of human experience.

The goal is 'to explore the religious dimension of human experience, to discover in faith the reality of God co-present in human experience, to situate the gracious revelation of God to the person within experience, to ground the activity of faith as a response to the experience of God and to live life more fully by participating passionately in the revelatory orientation of human experience. God comes to us in experience. We receive God in experience.

> We do not project, create or posit God in experience. Rather we find God already there, within and ahead of us, in human exper-ience.'14

This is such a profound revelation, with immediate implications for the way we live each moment of our lives both as Christians and as human beings in community.

Many of the tensions today in the life of the church are caused by a mis-understanding about the nature of revelation. 'Good theology is indis-pensable to the life of the church. It is informed by a searching fidelity to God's revelation in Christ available to us in scripture and the living tradition of the church. Theology in the normal course of events assumes the existence and givenness of revelation. For that reason theo-logy is as strong or as weak as its understanding of revelation is.'15

There is a disturbing apathy and widespread indifference towards theo-logy and faith today. This is leading to the almost total loss of the tran-scendent dimension of life and the search for truth. When this happens the community of faith must engage in a serious process of self-criti-cism. The question must be faced why there is indifference to that which is universal, human and in keeping with our deepest aspirations. 'Does the problem lie with the indifferent', Lane asks, 'or is it perhaps with that which the indifferent are being invited to respond to by the community of faith and the mediators of faith in that community? This particular question becomes all the more acute when we bear in mind that every individual has a natural capacity for God, that all have been graced by God *ab initio* with a corresponding real effect in their hearts, and that God is already revealed to the world in the person of Jesus of Nazareth. Is it possible, perhaps, that the indifferent have only been offered *beliefs* when it was *faith* they were searching for? Are we giving people stones of information when they are longing for the bread of wisdom?'16

It is no exaggeration to say that a theology of nature and grace, of creation and incarnation has led, for centuries, a lonely existence on the margins of our common theology. Its potential – its vast potential to infuse a much-needed energy and vibrancy into an often bloodless, doctrinaire theology – has remained unexplored. It is only in recent decades, part-icularly in the efforts made to release the treasures of Vatican II into the mainstreams of Catholic teaching and thinking, that the possibility of a new wave of renewal can be detected here and there. It will restore a clear dynamic of graced self-awareness to a confused church.

This chapter offers a sketch of one theological theme in OWTWL. It leads on to a vital theology of church, of sacraments, of sin and of redemption. I've heard teachers, impatient for the practical language of transmitting the faith in an increasingly complex society, say that they have already 'done' such Vatican II theology. Many, of course, have. Yet not all knowledge is just for transitory information. There is a knowing that transforms us; a knowing that also enters our hearts, even our bodies and our very being; a kind of knowing that is an echo of our own innate capacity for wisdom and beauty. We resonate with it. It disturbs us, entraps us and changes us. 'To understand the world,' wrote Teilhard de Chardin, 'knowledge is not enough. You must see it, touch it, live in its presence and drink the vital heat of existence in the very heart of humanity.' This understanding makes us strain to attain to further horizons. And this enfleshed wisdom demands to be shared.

To understand the world, knowledge is not enough.

It seems to me that pointers towards catechetical methodologies are already becoming evident within the underlying theology of nature and grace. When we have grasped and interiorised, even in vague outline, the Vatican II vision of some of these mysteries, the way forward will gradually clarify itself. The goal of the document's vision will not be achieved by inserting, or 'bolting on', new catechetical material to what we already have. A 'new mind', a transformation of consciousness, is what is called for. Once we let our imaginations free to play, and work with, a sacramental vision of both our supreme destiny and our valiant efforts to attain to it, then the Mystery of Life will move unerringly before us.

Many catechists, teachers and headteachers confess to being profoundly aware of, often embarrassed and alarmed by, their lack of theological expertise. This is not an unsurmountable situation. When the students are ready the teacher will come! A serious effort on their part is called for to keep in touch with the best of current writing; to avail themselves of every opportunity to be more deeply nourished by the best theological insights. That, in fact, is partly what OTWTL is about. And every effort must be made by our church authorities from now on, to facilitate and resource this vital adult education in theology. But excessive fear about dogmatic accuracy, for instance, on the part of catechists and teachers, will only reduce God to the limits of their own memories, and will strangle the essence of their graced imagination. The heart has its wisdom that dogma knows not of!

There is a *sensus fidelium*, a priesthood and holiness in the 'eternity of the heart'. Cardinal Hume often pointed out that we already carry within our 'naturally spiritual hearts' the outline plot of the Great Story. The essential *magisterium* carries a great respect for these human intuitions, for our honest speculation and imagination, for people's freedom to express, as church, what the Holy Spirit is saying to them. It knows that when everyone is thinking the same way, no one is thinking very much. When Pope Pius XII was preparing his Encyclical *Mystici Corporis* he told educators and preachers: 'When you're teaching about the Body of Christ, do not be afraid to exaggerate, because it is impossible to exaggerate so great a mystery!' What is needed in our own day is trust and courage – and imagination!

Theological Points

Here are some theological check-points to hold on to in our courageous conversations about the way forward for Catholic schools and parishes.

- Everything which is not God owes its existence to God. Created beings are distinct from God, though they may be, and in humanity have been, given a destiny which makes them more God-like. The Christian mystical tradition allows one to speak of 'sharing in God's being' or of 'deification'. Later theologians speak of 'panentheism' – an indwelling of God in men and women, and they in God. Both of these mystical traditions, when properly understood, safeguard divine transcendence.

- All creation is good. This doctrine negates a Gnostic dualism which sees the soul as good and the body as bad so as to account for the existence of evil in the created world. Strains of a similar type of Jansenism are still detectable in Christian teaching and preaching today.

- Although grace may be treated as a conceptual abstraction, it is concretely grounded in graced persons, events and things. There is no such thing as a grace which is grace and nothing else. Sound sacramental theology depends on a recognition of graced creation. If we wish to discover and encounter grace we must turn to the created world, because it is the created world which supplies the occasions that become the vehicles of grace.

- The doctrines of creation and redemption should be developed together and in a way that recognises the feedback of one into the other. Salvation is not an afterthought; it is antecedent to the 'sin of Adam' and to the commission of personal sin. It is implicit in the creation of a truly free being. When the created universe arrives at hominisation, it becomes an arena for salvation. To be human is to be wounded, incomplete, from the start. A perfect Adam and Eve never actually lived on planet earth!

- Christ is central to the whole divine economy, which includes creation, revelation and salvation. Every human being is in need of redemption.
- The incarnation is the paradigm in which human nature is permanently transformed through its union with the divine in the person of Jesus Christ. The bedrock of the Vatican Conciliar point of view is Christological. It is this perspective which is to be applied to the perennial theme of the relationship between nature and grace. As OTWTL emphases, grace is freely given but it is also an integral part of human nature, giving humanity its fundamental orientation to perfection in God, and accounting for the dynamic element of human nature which pushes it to seek that fulfilment, even if at times it looks for it in inappropriate places.
- This perspective also gives a theological basis for a Christ-centred humanism. Contemporary culture claims humanity as its own and makes it the measure of itself. Vatican II proposes an understanding of humanity which accepts what contemporary culture has to say about it in part, but completes it with the rich vision of humanity and its history transformed in Christ. Human beings and their culture, then, OTWTL affirms, may be seen as sacramental, finite realities which display the being of God because God has made his dwelling in them.
- However we may interpret the doctrine of original sin, there is no doubt about its reality in our lives. As individuals and as community we all carry a mysterious darkness within us, a sinister tendency towards evil. 'Man therefore is divided in himself. As a result, the whole life of men, both individual and social, shows itself to be a struggle, and a dramatic one, between good and evil, between light and darkness.' (*Gaudium et spes*, 13)
- The church calls us to a deeper sense of the mystery of life, of our interdependence with all of creation. Each one of us carries within us the fourteen billion year history of the cosmos. Young people are often aware that this sacred and fragile mystery is seriously threatened by ecological disaster, planetary death and human disintegration. Their faith is not dead. It may be buried from disillusionment – but it is not dead.
- Young people, too, are well aware that the marginalised of our world stand in the centre of the Good News. The way of Jesus is not the way of elitism and privilege.

- Christians are called to stay true to the divine voice within their own hearts, to the original vision of their birth and baptism. Only when they are faithful to the power of the indwelling Trinity will they be fearless prophets of the reign of God. Especially today, Christians need great courage to stay on fire with God's dream in them for what Pope John Paul II calls 'a new springtime for the church' and for the world.
- The Holy Spirit will not be locked away into any one church, and one form of religion. Until we believe that divine revelation is happening everywhere, we can never be truly ecumenical. Christianity, as Vatican II reminded us, 'rejects nothing which is true and holy in all religions.' (*Nostra Aetate*, 5)
- Now is the acceptable time. And only prayer will see us through. We pray, for a start, 'to act justly, to love tenderly, and to walk humbly with our God'.
- Karl Rahner was asked on German television in 1976: 'Could you briefly formulate the purpose and theme of your book *Foundations of Christian Faith?* Nicholas Lash used his reply as a conclusion to his own book *Holiness, Speech and Silence:* 'I only want to tell the reader something very simple. Human persons in every age, always and everywhere, whether they realise and reflect upon it or not, are in relationship with the unutterable mystery of human life that we call God. Looking at Jesus Christ the crucified and risen one, we can have the hope that now in our present lives, and finally after death, we will meet God as our own fulfilment.'(p 93)

Summary

We welcome a theology of nature and grace that honours the unlimited possibilities of humanity, intrinsically graced at its centre from the beginning.

This theology has radical implications for our own personal spirituality and for our work as parents, teachers, catechists and priests.

Human nature is intrinsically ordered to God; humanity and history are transformed in Christ; the alchemist's stone is Christ. (OTWTL)

However we may interpret the doctrine of original sin, there is absolutely no doubt about its reality in our lives and in our world. But while it may be all-pervasive, it is never all-victorious.

To explore the mystery of incarnation knowledge is not enough; a 'new mind', a transformation of consciousness is needed.

Incarnation has a cosmic significance that is celebrated in the Eucharist. *(John Paul II)*

Vatican II proposes an understanding of humanity which accepts what contemporary culture has to say about it in part, but completes it with the rich vision of humanity and its history transformed in Christ. (OTWTL)

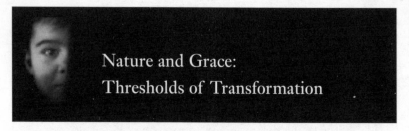

Nature and Grace:
Thresholds of Transformation

Theologian Karl Rahner wished to move away from a familiar dichotomy between nature and grace that is still emphasised in our churches. Our whole lives, by virtue of creation and incarnation, are graced by God's own self-expression from the beginning, whether or not this astonishing revelation is ever articulated. The teacher, the priest, the catechist and the formator need to be thoroughly 'inside' this kind of theology. They need to be comfortable with the wisdom that sees God as the absolute and loving mystery now insinuated into the innermost core of humanity. The catechist reveals to people that they are already grasped by God's graced self-revelation in the hiddeness and ordinariness of their everyday lives.

Education is more about revealing than transmitting.

Education is more about revealing than transmitting. In a Christian context, it is about revealing the presence of God hidden within our lives and within the world. This is the aim of all catechesis, formation, liturgical celebration and religious education. If this is the overall goal of all true evangelical ministry, then it is vital that the workers in the vineyard should be well appraised of the theological basis for holding this view. The ministry of teaching is not so much to facilitate God's 'breaking into' a profane world at certain particular points, as to help people to experience the 'breaking out' of God's own self, already and always present at the heart of the world.

There are many theologians to choose from, but Karl Rahner is particularly helpful in clarifying the issues here. He would see the enterprise of education as that of alerting people to the fact that, whether they are aware of it or not, whether they accept or repress it, they all have 'an experience of grace from within'. With human experience as the subject, he places this goal as the most original and important one in the work of Christianity.

Our students, fundamentally, are open to everything. This openness, as many teachers will attest to, may not always be obvious! Rahner sees the human heart as always restless, never satisfied. As people continue to examine and question their experiences and to enlarge their horizons of understanding, under the attractive force of their own restless search and of God's Spirit, they reveal themselves to be people of those 'unlimited horizons' that catalyse the drive for absolute fulfilment.

This understanding of the work of the teacher changes everything. It introduces to the discipline an excitement, a challenge and a nobility that we have all but forgotten. The task is to identify, nourish and set free those 'deeper realities of the spirit'. We are moving in another world of love and meaning when we believe that God is the foundational impulse behind every attraction to know truth, to love goodness, to be drawn to beauty. The exploration of life itself then, whether in the young pupil preparing for First Communion, or in the formation of the adult RCIA candidate, provides the necessary threshold into the spiritual treasure in every human heart.

God is the foundational impulse behind every attraction to know truth, to love goodness, to be drawn to beauty.

Rahner wished to move away from a persistent church dichotomy between nature and grace that was emphasised in past centuries. It still is. Our whole lives, by virtue of creation and incarnation, are graced by God's own self-expression from the beginning, whether or not this astonishing revelation is ever articulated. In fact to facilitate such articulation is the most urgent calling of those who evangelise, catechise and preach. The divisive curse of dualism gives way to the healing blessing of divine indwelling.

In the unitive vision of nature and grace, the transcendent reality of God's mystery and of infinite horizons are in no way threatened. But those who honour their openness in faith 'experience rather that this holy mystery (God's otherness) is also a hidden closeness, a forgiving intimacy, their real home; that it is a love that shares itself, something familiar which they can approach and turn to from the estrangement of their own perilous and empty lives'.[17] Is not this the transformation that the well-meaning gurus and healers of our time are continually promising to provide for the lost souls of our searching people today? Sometimes, to an extent, they succeed. It is time to rediscover the power of our Christian story for bringing a new abundance into the lives of those we serve; a new vision for a searching society.

The teacher, the priest and the formator need to be thoroughly 'inside' this kind of theology. They need to be comfortable with the wisdom that sees God as the absolute mystery whose historical self-communication in creation and in incarnation has insinuated God's own essence into the innermost core of our humanity. The catechist reveals to people that they are grasped by God's graced self-revelation in the hiddeness and ordinariness of their humanity. To do this requires many communicating skills and much inner authority on the part of the facilitator. It is not easy to acquire the vision; it is difficult to spread it, to make it work. The ever-present shadow of original sin falls over everything. And the meeting-place between heaven and earth will always be paradoxical and subtle. The discerning eyes of compassion are needed here. The French philosopher Blaise Pascal has reminded us of the mystery of 'our greatness as transcendent spirit and our smallness as finite, limited, but receptive beings.'

The teacher will remember those special times when the totally unaware student first begins to glimpse something of the stunning bigger picture of God's destiny for us all. Yet even 'the totally unaware' student is, to some extent, already open to this possible unfolding, ready for a long time to grow into a clearer understanding of the mystery of her humanity, to enter and inhabit her true home. Some theologians refer to such times as 'the mystical moment' when the first gifts of the Spirit actually bear fruit in the soul – wisdom, understanding, knowledge. It is then that the journey in faith truly begins, as the mystical moments grow more frequent, and each new step provides a clearer glimpse of yet another summit to freely and gladly fill our attention.

The teacher's task is to recognise the heart of God in the heart of life, to reveal the divine presence active in all human presences, to decipher God's signature written indelibly but often faintly, across all of creation. This vision, established once-for-all in the incarnation, is continually renewed within the soul of the world by the Holy Spirit. And the church and sacraments testify to the truth and eternity of that vision. It is all of a piece. Everything belongs. We need eyes to see the integrity and profound simplicity of God's incredibly beautiful plan for the world. We are encompassed in a warm embrace way beyond our wildest dreams. Only our creative imaginations can begin to lay hold of this shy mystery.

The End of Dualism

Catechists and teachers often lose confidence in, and patience with, obscure theologies and distracting dogmas that confuse their aims and energies. They wait for some kind of enabling clarity to facilitate and inspire their commitment. The greatest blinkers and blockage to the effective and satisfying exercise of their special profession is the subtle dualism that often runs through the current pastoral practice of 'hand-

The catechist reveals to people that they are grasped by God's graced self-revelation in the hiddeness and ordinariness of their humanity.

ing on the faith'. It is the single most destructive element obstructing their holy work because it strikes at the very heart of what Jesus came to accomplish. Fearfully, it persists in keeping rent, the costly, precious and organic fabric of creation and Creator – that fabric that Jesus, in his own body, had established as forever carefully and lovingly woven together. Nor is there any reason to fear that God is diminished in the graced elevation of creation and humanity.

God is not diminished in the graced elevation of creation and humanity.

None of the theologians we are relying on in these pages will have any truck with dualism. True to scripture, Rahner refuses to separate the world of grace from the world of nature. He agrees with Aquinas about the graced nature of creation from the very beginning. Many neo-scholastic textbook theologies and catechisms have seriously distorted God's desire to be intimately associated with us in the humanity of Jesus. This distortion has been reinforced by a catechesis that sees grace as something almost material to be poured into receptive souls, but only when they were deserving and worthy. In contemporary, truly incarnational theology God's nearness makes possible a graced transformation of human understanding. God presents to creatures a beckoning horizon of love and meaning to which people aspire in their conscious and unconscious search for fulfilment.

God is intrinsically present in God's people, enabling them to experience themselves as included in the inner life of God. Augustine's *noverim me noverim te* is a testimony to that belief. He searched for self-knowledge so as to be nearer to God. As intimate as he was with his own essence, God's own self was closer still. Teachers and catechists need to be confident enough to reject any understanding of grace that sees it as a higher kind of layer laid very carefully on top of the layer of nature, with no interpenetration between the two.

Grace and nature are inseparable. There is an original unity and intimacy between the experience of self and the experience of God to the extent that the history of one becomes the history of the other. Rahner claims that

'the experience of self is the condition which makes it possible to experience God.'

It is clear from the gospel that in the love of neighbour one has already discovered God. Our human experience is the medium through which revelation takes place. That is why it is in the unfolding of our lives that the eternal plan of God is revealed in each one of us. Through the gift of grace, people are immersed in God's presence, inspirited by God's love, and filled with a sense of their common destiny. In this union with Christ they are fulfilled by God alone. 'There cannot be two parallel lives in our existence – on the one hand the so-called spiritual life and on the other, the so-called secular life.' (Introduction to RC National Syllabus 'Here I Am'.)

Scandal of Particularity

Rahner writes: 'We want, as far as possible, to experience the reality of grace in our own existence where we experience ourselves; we want to see and feel its power at work within us. And in accordance with other modern tendencies, we shall want to see grace not only as it concerns the individual, but also ... grace in the history of salvation not only within the church but in the possibility of grace and its highest manifestations in the world of non-Christian religions.'[18] And, we might add, in the whole universe and in the cosmos itself.

The notion of 'the scandal of particularity' applies to the enfleshing of God in the particular person of Jesus at a particular time and place. It is regarded by many as a scandal because it is so historically defined and specific. Many are more comfortable with a vague, removed deity. There is also a kind of scandal of particularity about the continuing incarnation of God in all of us, at all times and in all places. Beyond knowledge of God we seek the personal impact of God's presence. And this is how it is in the divine economy of salvation. God communicates God's self to human beings in their own reality, in the ebb and flow of their lives, in the horizons they reach and in the dreams that may never see the light of day. This is the mystery and the fullness of grace in the here and now. It is a mystery with profound implications for our teaching, catechesis and preaching.

We can see that the emphasis of OTWTL on finding appropriate language for the accurate transmission of our faith-story is not a secondary concern.

> It belongs to the very essence of the incarnation that it should be revealed as being for all people at all times; as being fully applicable and identifiable within the panorama of the whole world and the minute details of each person's life. There is no exception.

The good news of the gospel is not a white Western commodity that can be transported around the world and inserted into, or laid on top of, other societies and cultures. In our local communities, with their rich varieties of ethnic minorities, a huge challenge awaits those pastoral ministers who are called and eager to reveal the wonderful story of our origins, our destinies and our multi-faceted journeys along the way. The good news needs to be received within the context of each one's particular environment, language, images and experiences.

Even in a secularist world a creation-centred, incarnational theology is compelling news for all who wish to live their lives as fully as possible. God's revelation in Jesus Christ assures us of our wider and deeper context. It is perfectly acceptable, our theologians assure us, to hold that humanity's whole essence and existence is permanently penetrated by grace. Just because grace is free and unmerited, they claim, does not mean that it is rare. Teaching, catechising and preaching is the awakening and making explicit of what is already there in the heart of humans by virtue of the already graced nature of all creation.

No matter how people may try, they can never escape from this holy enfolding. And no matter how they may wish to think otherwise, it is to this hidden destiny that they are irrevocably and insistently called. Often beyond conscious awareness of it, all human beings experience a longing and a yearning for union with that from which they have issued forth, and to which they will inevitably return. In a sense they have no choice in the matter.

Human beings can be understood in their undeniable essence only when seen as the graced potential for union with the divine life. 'Who is to say,' asks Rahner, 'that the voice heard in earthly philosophy, even non-Christian and pre-Christian philosophy, is the voice of nature alone (and perhaps of nature's guilt) and not also the groaning of the creature, who is already moved in secret by the Holy Spirit of grace, and longs, without realising it, for the glory of the children of God?'[19] Teaching and preaching is about bringing a new consciousness to people who seek a richer understanding of what is happening in their lives and in the world.

Teaching and preaching is about bringing a new consciousness to people who seek a richer understanding of what is happening in their lives and in the world.

Ordinary Mystical Thresholds

St Paul's prayer for us to 'put on Christ', to have 'the mind of Christ', is substantially answered when we learn to see things sacramentally. To look at anything in the light of incarnation is to notice the 'surplus of meaning', the 'excess of significance' in what is going on around us. The work of evangelising is like bringing colour into what was only black and white before. It is about completing what is already hinted at. There was an advert for motor cars some years ago which consisted of a manuscript page from one of Mozart's compositions. The caption read, 'It remains only dots and squiggles – until you play it.' Catechising is like that. It reveals something deeper. It is like what happens when we bring those 'magic-eye' books close to our faces and then, when our focus softens, what at first were formless curves and vague shapes become breathtaking vistas, or deep-sea revelations. It is a journey of discovery into the veiled temples of our ordinary experiences; an exploration into the rich veins of a deeper truth about the value and worth of what happens every day.

There is a hint of mysticism in such an understanding of spreading the word. Let this not alarm anyone. The meaning of mysticism needs to be de-mythologised!

> We are all mystics – either potentially or actually. The teacher and preacher, above all, need to keep their mystical hearts nourished.

By reflecting on the marvellous love-story of God's dream for us, by touching God in the bits and pieces of each day, by breathing into the creative activity of the Blessed Trinity deep within her, by setting her imagination free to roam across the countryside of possibilities, the catechist will be nurtured and motivated into an ever-increasing cycle of wisdom and delight.

A theology of nature and grace discerns the unrestricted movement of the Holy Spirit wherever people are committed to genuine human values and humanitarian pursuits. It would identify the longing for God in all human longing. It would identify God's Spirit ranging across the whole spectrum of creation, of history and of individual experiences, in ways far beyond the constricted and limited places, people and things to which many of our textbook theologies and catechisms would restrict it. Rahner, for instance, recognises the activity of the Spirit within every attraction towards expansion, breakthrough, pursuit of the good, and hoping against hope. All of these aspirations and drives are not just examples of the work of the Spirit but true experiences of the very essence of God. These movements and restless impulses to be fulfilled and to be part of a bigger horizon result from the stirring and motivating of a passionate, beckoning God. We are reflecting here on the mysticism of everyday life.

The mysticism of everyday life.

The work of forming people in the Christian faith is to convince them of the closeness of God to them, and of the ever-present temptation to repress, ignore or resist that inner conviction. The preacher or teacher will always be searching for ways of revealing that this mysticism, this vague awareness of transcendence, this sensing of the divine in the midst, is already the work of the Spirit within each one – a Spirit that is somehow incarnated and contained in the most ordinary, sober and secular experience in the normal course of everyday life. Because there is something fundamentally simple at the heart of this kind of theology, there are very successful ways to hand for enabling both child and adult to rejoice in such revelation. However, most of our curricula and programmes need some radical revising because some of that deep simplicity is getting lost in over-elaborate schemes or knowledge-based approaches due, perhaps, to an unclear theology of revelation, and its immediate effect on the way we live each day.

The thrust of what is being said here holds true whether we are concerned with normal, in-faith, pastoral catechesis or RE, with dialogue with those of other faiths, or with the evangelising of religionless seekers of a more abundant life. And one thing is for sure. The teacher who is enchanted by this vision of things, who is living out in her own life the wonder and freedom afforded by these revelations about God's intimate indwelling at the heart of our lives, will never be short of persuasive and compelling stories, images, moments and little miracles to draw her listeners to thresholds in their own lives too. Her life itself will become a beacon of attraction. The hours of God's grace are always and everywhere to hand and to heart.

A Piece of Homework!

This homework is by way of preparation for a central issue that will be explored more fully in Part Three. This issue concerns our catechetical aims and how we select our material in the teaching process so as to achieve those aims. Are our aims, for instance, to do with a knowledge of the faith or to do with bringing about a transformation of each student through an awareness and experience of a relationship with God? An example may help.

In line with the best principles of current faith-centred pedagogy, many of our most enlightened school syllabuses, catechetical programmes and RCIA guidelines have one thing in common – they try to begin with the actual experiences of those involved. This is the right start. However, after a few lessons into this lively process of reflection and exploration of life, the momentum too often drifts away into another place. The promising, life-centred interchange about topics such as relationships, emotions, seasons and senses may easily be lost sight of and another agenda creeps in and takes over. The original vision becomes blurred, the follow-through wavers. The focus may now begin to be excessively directed towards measurable knowledge and repeatable formulations.

Having perused, and tried to teach within the structure and sequence of such themes, I have found the connection between the opening, exciting, interactive work, and the consequent development, to be often tenuous and not intrinsically of a piece. This second part of the pedagogical exercise usually has to do with knowledge about God and Jesus, or with a better understanding of the sacraments, or with more thorough information about aspects of the Christian and Catholic faith. While the contents and benefits of this secondary agenda are utterly necessary, many concerned Catholic voices today fear that the hoped-for spiritual impact of the Christian faith on the very quality and daily reality of students' lives is less than it should be. Something central is 'lost in translation' so to speak. Especially in the complex, multicultural world of young and old today.

The process, to be true to God's story as revealed in a theology of nature and grace, would stay with the initial exploration of the students' lives right through to the end of the unit. As Rahner and other theologians are at pains to point out, it is precisely, and only, 'in the digging into the rubble of our lives (the life-theme) that the gold of God (the implications of incarnation for that particular piece of ground) is found'. If God comes to us, according to Von Balthasar, disguised as our lives, then it must be in the penetration of that 'secular' disguise that God's face is revealed. If, according to St John Chrysostom, the key that fits the human heart unlocks the heart of God as well, then it is in our inner awareness that we grasp, however vaguely, something of the nature of God.

If God comes to us, according to Von Balthasar, disguised as our lives, then it must be in the penetration of that 'secular' disguise that God's face is revealed.

What implications does this insight have for the way we approach our Christian educational work in all its forms? In the following pages we continue to address this question.

Summary

Education is more about revealing than transmitting.........
The good news can only be received within the context of each one's particular environment, language, images and experiences. Where catechesis is concerned, one size never fits all. Each individual heart, in its own personal truth and reality, is invited to respond.
God is not diminished in the graced elevation of humanity and creation.
The hours of God's grace are always and everywhere close to hand and to heart.
Teachers and catechists need to keep their mystical hearts nourished.
The deep simplicity of the sacramental vision is often distorted or lost due to over-elaborate and doctrine-based schemes. There is a need for a re-visioning of our religious education, catechesis and preaching.
Whether they know and accept it or not, all students have an experience of grace from within.

Sacrament Revisited:
Prisms of Revelation

The way in which we understand faith will determine the way we do theology and it will also shape the character of our Christian education in all its forms. If we regard faith as mainly to do with learning, knowing and believing many doctrines and propositions, then theology and catechesis will be understood and presented in terms of such concerns. Where faith, on the other hand, is understood as a response to the mystery of the incarnation, of God's immediacy in human experience, then theology and Christian education will take the form of an exploration of that same human experience, in a way that illuminates and reveals the active, enlightening mystery of God at the heart of the world. The notion of 'sacrament' is central to our understanding and spreading of the Christian faith.

Within the horizons of the theology of nature and grace considered here, there is a basic theology of sacrament without which we will always struggle to understand and teach the Christian faith. Once we make that central ground of revealed truth our own, then we will have immense confidence and consistency in the way we approach our teaching and catechising. What follows is an effort to explore this central Christian notion of sacrament, beginning with Christ, the primal sacrament, with a view to its presentation in the work of catechesis.

Jesus – the Human One, Sacrament of God

The seeds of a theology of nature and grace were sown on the first Pentecost Sunday. The gifts of the Holy Spirit were already expanding the hearts of the disciples with a new understanding of the meaning of the birth, death and resurrection of Jesus. Above all, what was gripping their imagination was the fact that it was in his humanity that he achieved what he had to achieve. The transformation of their lives was brought about by the truth of their friendship with this ordinary, extraordinary man. At a high level of intimacy – because, in a sense, their very lives were at stake – they shared their deepest doubts, hopes, fears and expectations with their new and very human friend. They were called, forgiven, and captivated by him. Their world was turned around by him. And at the end of it all, after the terrible trauma of his death, and their confused experiences of his resurrection, something amazing began to dawn on them. To know him, they now realised, was to know God. To walk, in love, with him was to walk, in love, with God. In the company of Jesus they had confided in, touched and embraced God-made-flesh. That is why Edward Schillebeeckx called Jesus 'the primordial sacrament of the encounter with God'.

Jesus 'the primordial sacrament of the encounter with God'.

The Spirit of Pentecost inspired them to grasp the fact that what was true of Jesus was true of everyone. God was now, incredibly, as accessible as any true human encounter. Jesus first, and then the church, became the sacrament of universal salvation. This is something we must learn in a new way. In solidarity with Jesus, everyone is a sacrament of God. Because every detail of Jesus' humanity shone out with divine grace, so it is with us. Because Jesus, to be truly human, would have to have experienced all human emotion, then all human emotion is potentially revelatory of God. Put another way, it was God's desire that the divine essence and splendour should be fully revealed in the finite, real humanity of a man called Jesus – Jesus, the Human One.

> In more theological language, the story goes like this. Jesus is not just the bearer of revelation; he *is* the revelation. Revelation is more than a series of truths about God; it is a human being.

He is, in his humanity, the message he brings. Jesus does not merely utter words about God; he himself *is* the uttered word. The humanity of Jesus is the summit and full reality of the yearnings of both creation and of God. Every moment of his life was an invitation to his disciples, and to us, to become more completely human. Always open to love, he himself never compromised. To discover what humanity ought to be, what it can be, the Christian looks at Jesus because he reveals, and indeed is, both the very fullness of created being, and of God-become-human. His is the humanity against which we all measure the truth of our lives. That all of us, like him, already God's children, may become even more Godlike, is the purpose of life (1 Jn 3:2)

Full of this dynamic vision of the meaning of Christ's humanity then and now, the committed teacher or catechist will find new energy for unfolding the relevance for her students. No detail of their lives will be excluded from the constant discovery and offer of grace. Whatever excites them, frightens them, confuses them will be the central subject matter of a faith-discussion about Jesus (or, for that matter, about any central aspect of the Christian faith). The reason for holding to this view is that if revelation is about God – a God who desires the fullness of intimacy with us – then equally it must be about humanity, for Christ is both the reality of God's desire for us, and of our full acceptance of that desire. The locus and moment of revelation and salvation then, takes place in the living experience of humanity and its meaning, in the light of Christ.

Jesus, the sacrament of God, was so thoroughly and utterly human that he scandalised his neighbours more than once. John the Baptist came fasting and they said he was possessed. Jesus came eating and drinking and they called him a glutton and a drunkard. He showed his anger, his deep desire, his need of male and female company, his frustration and his impatience – 'Get behind me Satan,' and 'How long have I been with you and yet, you have learned so little!' This is the humanity that has opened heaven to us (Heb 5:1-10). In his finite condition, Jesus took on the three great sufferings of physical pain, a loss of his good name, and a sense of ultimate abandonment by his father. He also laughed, cried, rejoiced, befriended, loved, was tempted, was intimate, celebrated, needed to rest, enjoyed eating and drinking. He confronted evil, and above all, confronted the dark night of his own soul. He was betrayed by one he deeply loved. He grew in wisdom and age and grace.

> Jesus, the sacrament of God, was thoroughly and utterly human.

At this point, anticipating some reflections more fully expanded in the final chapters of this book, I draw attention to two of them. The first is this. Since it was in the humanity of Jesus, his human friendship, his expression of his emotions, that people experienced God, it is to the purification of our own humanity that we must dedicate our lives if we are ever to be 'other Christs' as we are all called to be. It is precisely with our authentic, vulnerable humanity that people can identify.

> Just as it was in the humanity of Jesus that God revealed God's own essence and unconditional love, so too it is through our humanity that God continues to reveal the divine pity and compassion to others.

And just as Jesus had to enter into the desert of his own heart, and face his own temptations, demons and shadows thus experiencing and expressing his true humanity and therefore divinity, so we too need to spend contemplative time in the shadow places of our own lives if we are ever to be credible and worthy teachers and preachers of the word.

The second reflection is a reminder that the enterprise of catechesis will always follow the pattern of the incarnation. 'Begin with the human heart!' said Meister Eckhart, many centuries ago. The underlying motif of all our catechesis and preaching has to begin with aspects of creation and dimensions of our humanity (as Jesus' approach always did) and then to reveal and disclose how, in the light of revelation, these realities and experiences are purified, intensified and celebrated in the Christian way of life.

> That pattern of beginning with the exploration of the human condition, of then revealing its potential transformation in the incarnation, and finally of sustaining and celebrating this new creation will always characterise Christian catechesis.

In this way, a theology of nature and grace becomes the inspiration for a fresh approach to teaching in all its forms. This approach will never stray too far from its incarnation-based, creation-centred and humanity-focused catechesis of life. The basically simple threefold movement of this approach will be examined again in Part Three.

Tout est Grace

As we explore the profound implications for our work of a theology of nature and grace, and as we reflect on the fundamental notion of 'sacrament', a word on 'grace' itself is appropriate. Even before Vatican II, through the patient work of scholars such as Marechal, de Lubac, Congar and Fransen, the institutional restrictions on grace were beginning to be lifted. No longer mediated solely by the church, the reality of grace was revealed to be multi-dimensional, encompassing ontological, psychological and social aspects of humanity. Moreover, this reality is shown as truly incarnational in that it is present to all people as the fundamental motivator of love, the ultimate condition of all goodness in the world. 'All of this (the graced offer of salvation) holds true not only for Christians but for all people of goodwill in whose hearts grace works in an unseen way. For, since Christ died for all, and since the ultimate vocation of humanity is in fact one and divine, we ought to believe that God's Spirit, in a manner known only to God, offers to everyone the possibility of being associated with the paschal mystery.'[20]

Grace refers to that significant ground of all being which circumscribes and supports the horizon and depth of all everyday experience. Grace is the innate capacity to relate, forgive, overcome suffering, create, sacrifice, imagine, explore – indeed to do anything which is a positive option for love and growth. It is more than that. It is what makes us who we are. 'Properly speaking we do not receive grace; we do not possess it as something foreign to us, or as something entering us from the outside; no, we *are* our grace.'[21]

There is bound to be a transformation in the catechising of those who understand grace in this way. They catch the wonderful essence of a theology of grace and nature. 'Grace,' writes Rahner, 'is simply the last depth and the radical meaning of all that the created person experiences, enacts, suffers in the process of developing and realising himself as a person. When someone experiences laughter or tears, bears responsibility, stands by the truth, breaks through the egoism in his life with other people; where someone hopes against hope, faces the shallowness and stupidity of the daily rush and bustle with humour and patience, refusing to become embittered; where someone learns to be silent and in this inner silence lets the evil in his heart die rather than spread outwards; in a word, wherever someone lives as he would like to live, combating his own egoism and the continual temptation to inner despair – there is the event of grace.'[22]

The death of Jesus was partly a punishment by the religious of his time for the way he disempowered all ecclesiastical elitism by short-circuiting it as the source of grace. He was killed because he made God's grace too accessible – as accessible as the next conversation, the next event, the next thought, the next breath. When grace is everywhere freely available, the religious institutions and authorities lose their control, and therefore their power. What Jesus was saying was quite shocking and, to some of his listeners, blasphemous. It is equally shocking today, but, for some reason, while its meaning was never more true and needed, its impact is being perennially blunted and resisted.

> Any teacher or preacher who really believes that God's vibrant presence is pressing in on every side, from outside in and from inside out, has no option but to be transformed by this revelation, and, at every pastoral session, to transform those around the desk or table.

This is astounding good news. It sets hearts on fire. It sends people out into the night with a new hope. It fills people, as they return home, with gratitude and wonder. Grace is life fully lived.

Theologian James Mackey puts it this way: 'The life which is now being called God's grace to man (*sic*) is precisely the life of everyone's everyday experience. It is man's working and eating, walking in the fields or on the seashore, playing for his team or dancing in his club, sleeping with his wife or talking with his friends, suffering the slings and arrows of outrageous fortune or holding out a helping hand to his neighbour, deciding what is best with the best guidance he can get, and getting up for Mass on Sundays. All that is grace.'[23]

The work of evangelising and catechising is about naming the place of grace for our young and older students. This is what Jesus did. He revealed the holiness of every aspect of people's lives – especially in the unexpected places. He ended the dualism that saw grace as a kind of divine icing on a human cake. He revealed that creation and humanity are graced from the very beginning. He transformed people's consciousness of the meaning of the world, of their neighbours and of themselves. This was redemption. This was salvation. And it still is.

To break open for students of all ages the mysterious love and meaning that is hidden at the heart of their lives and of their experiences is to redeem and save them. To nourish people's souls with that one reality they were created to be nourished by is to bring about the new creation that Jesus died for. In the hands of the informed and passionate teacher or catechist, fired and sustained by the Holy Spirit's gifts of wisdom and understanding, a new dynamism will enter our churches, our schools and our world.

Sacrament and sacraments

From its very beginning, billions of years ago, the raw material of the world was already permeated and filled with God's subtle but powerful presence. There never was a time or space in the history of evolution when God was absent from this planet. In the person of Christ this tremendous love-story has been finally revealed.

> A new consciousness has enfolded the world. The human is now the home of the divine. The redemption has happened. What was begun in creation is finalised and revealed in the incarnation.

The Son is the completion of the Father's initiative. In Jesus we recognise the salvation that is already throbbing within us. It is divine power that energises our daily lives, that finds the summer of God's grace in the winters we must live through. The whole world is perceived as sacrament. This way of seeing things is called the sacramental vision. And it is this vision of the deepest reality that we celebrate in the sacraments. Without the wider sacramental vision, the sacraments themselves would lose their true meaning and become empty or even dead ritual. Given the relentless reality of our fallen nature, this possibility is always uncomfortably close.

Because, like the disciples in the Emmaus story, we tend to forget. The heavy clouds of original sin forever obscure the clarity of the divine

Without the wider sacramental vision, the sacraments themselves would lose their true meaning and become empty or even dead ritual.

presence all around us. It is in the fog of this blindness that we sin. We 'miss the mark', as scripture puts it, because we cannot see clearly anymore. We miss the mystery too. Our act of seeing stops at first appearances. Sin has no imagination. No longer is the smallest particle of creation a theophany of grace. No longer is every moment a revelation of eternity, of 'the dearest freshness deep down things'. Sin is blind. It is blind to beauty. It resists the light of openness. It controls by fear. It cannot bless or celebrate or be passionate about anything. It chooses to live in illusion and isolation. As Aquinas believed, sin is a 'defect in goodness'; it happens through a loss – the loss, it seems, of the sacramental vision.

In a striking paragraph, Fr Sean Fagan, Irish theologian and author, combines elements of the sacramental vision and sacramental celebration. The latter becomes more meaningful, he writes, 'when it is seen as a high-point, a peak moment, a special occasion in a life that is already sacramental in its own right. The sacraments are of a piece with the rest of life and reality, not eruptions from a different world. In this sense it is more helpful to approach them from the context of life as a whole. They are moments of insight, bringing home to us, each in its own way, the deeper meaning of our life and destiny. The sacraments declare forth what is otherwise hidden in the darkness of the world, in the routine of everyday. They bring into focus and draw our attention to what we tend to ignore and lose sight of, when we are busy about many things.'[24]

The sacraments are of a piece with the rest of life and reality, not eruptions from a different world.

We would be hard put to avoid the experience of God. It is practically inescapable. We cannot help coming into the embrace of the divine presence in all our experiences. In one of our current RE programmes, teachers are reminded that, 'We do not sometimes have experiences of love, fear, ourselves, or anything else, and then have experiences of God as well. The basic, original experience of God, on the contrary, is the ultimate depth and radical essence of *every* personal experience ...' Until this is clearly understood it is very difficult to grasp the essential role of the catechist or RE teacher.

An important part of their task will be to explain why Christians believe that their attitude to their experiences either nourishes or poisons that potential for friendship with God. Teilhard de Chardin points out: 'Through every cleft, the world we perceive floods us with riches – food for the body, nourishment for the eyes, the harmony of sounds and fullness of the heart, unknown phenomena and new truths – all these treasures, all these stimuli, all these calls coming to us from the four corners of the world, cross our consciousness at every moment. What is their role within us? They will merge into the most intimate life of our soul, and either develop or poison it.'[25]

Without this understanding it is difficult, too, to experience the true meaning of liturgical celebration. We looked at this in section three of Part One. If we cannot see God in the ordinary events of life, Rahner holds, then we cannot normally expect to suddenly experience God when we gather to worship. To the extent that we have a heightened awareness of the absolute mystery in all the joys and sufferings of life, will we have little trouble in finding God at the moment of the sacraments. The sacraments of the church make explicit what is implicit in the sacrament of the world.

The sacraments of the church make explicit what is implicit in the sacrament of the world.

'That which is lived out in an everyday manner outside the sacraments,' Schillebeeckx writes, 'grows to its full maturity in them. The anonymity of everyday Christian living is removed by the telling power of Christ's symbolic action in and through his church.'[26] He is convinced that we all carry a child-mystic within us; that mysticism, in its real meaning, is not as remote as we often assume; that Christians must become mystics who are attuned to the mysterious light that shines behind all that happens. The art of teaching is the art of liberating people into an enduring possession of who they already are. 'Make ready for Christ,' shouts Thomas Merton, 'whose smile, like lightning, sets free the song of everlasting glory that now sleeps, in your paper flesh, like dynamite.' This process begins and ends at the heart of life.

There is a happy coincidence of pedagogical and theological approaches to communication here in that the emphasis on child-centred and life-centred education in general is ideally suited to the particular thrust of a catechesis based on a theology of nature and grace. They both realise that the transformation of the whole person is what real education is about. Whether a particular discipline is drawn from the humanities or the sciences, the overall aim should be the enhancement of the total lives of the students – a dimension of the abundant life promised by Jesus.

That is why any consideration of Catholic 'ethos' must include the graced nature of the teaching of any subject, the liberating of the student into a wider and deeper understanding of any aspect of experience or creation. Whatever reveals some dimension of the essence and wonder of the world is also revealing something of the mystery of the Creator, of providing others with a sacramental vision of their lives. And this task of identifying God's presence in their most ordinary experiences, can only be carried out in the often-harsh reality of where people 'are at' in the here and now.

Summary

The notion of sacrament is central to our understanding and spreading of the Christian faith.

Jesus, the sacrament of God, was thoroughly and utterly human. It was in this fragile and finite humanity that God, from the beginning, desired to become flesh.

That is why the locus and moment of revelation continues to take place in the living experience of all people and in the unfailing existence of all creation.

What was begun in creation is finalised in incarnation.

Properly speaking we do not receive grace; we do not possess it as something from outside; no, we *are* our grace. Grace is life fully lived.

Without the wider sacramental vision, the seven sacraments themselves would lose their true meaning and become empty ritual.

The sacraments declare forth what is otherwise hidden in the darkness of the world, in the routine of every day.

Courageous Conversations

There are many theologies within the church. Can you name some of them?

Do you agree that theology is for living as well as for learning?

How does a theology of nature and grace transform your understanding of what it means to be a Christian? Do you resonate with this theology?

What difficulties do you have with this theology?

Do you understand how a theology of nature and grace does not replace a theology of sin and redemption but balances and underpins it; how there is both healing and completing in the life and work of Jesus?

In your own words, how would you tell someone about it? How would you describe the language needed to show to a secular society the realities of salvation, sin and the need for redemption?

How has Vatican II informed your understanding of the church?

Why is the reclaiming of the sacramental vision and imagination so crucial for catechesis and preaching in today's church?

Part Three

The Art of Educating

A theology of nature and grace suggests a three-fold education strategy. As in the basic pattern of creation, incarnation and mission, it is appropriate to identify and emphasise three fundamental stages of Christian education in our schools and parishes. In general terms, the first phase of any theme or topic looks at aspects of personal experience, creation and the human condition in the raw, so to speak. After the creative exploring by the students of these aspects and experiences, the transforming light shed on them by the birth and Passover of Jesus Christ is then shared. This is the good news that changes everything. All is revealed as already in God's image, already saved, but always in need of purification. The third phase is where the new awareness of this deeper love and meaning at the heart of students' lives and loves is remembered, rejoiced in, and celebrated in all kinds of ways. This is the awareness that, in turn, motivates and empowers the students with a sense of mission and service to the world.

Catholic stories are incarnational; they speak of God incarnate in the human condition. But the stories have been discarded in favour of the doctrines. The church exists to tell the stories. The story came before the doctrine. Doctrine grows from story and can never exhaust its truth. It is the beauty of the story that holds Catholics to their heritage. Beauty is not opposed to truth. It is simply truth in its most attractive form.

Andrew Greeley

Where there is much desire to learn, there of necessity will be much arguing, much writing, many opinions; for opinions in good people is but knowledge and wisdom in the making.

John Milton

The fruit of truth must grow and mature on the tree of the subject before it can be plucked and placed in its absolute realm.

Bernard Lonergan

The groundwork of religious education must relate the insights of theology and the philosophy of education. It must comprehend development psychology and the techniques of curriculum development. Its focus is a practical activity rather than an abstract theme.

Kevin Nichols

Any subject can be taught effectively in some intellectually honest form to any child at any age of development ... Teaching and learning is the enterprise *par excellence* where the line between subject-matter (content) and method (process) grows necessarily indistinct.

Jerome Bruner

I cannot imagine what else a teacher, or for that matter a preacher, should do, except to remind people of their capacity for the infinite ... that evincing of memory, that eliciting of nostalgia, that desire of the Spirit. All teachers know this humility, this diffidence in practice, for they know that when they have taught well the students will spontaneously say 'of course' – for they recognise, as if recalling a truth no longer the teacher's, because now commonly possessed and shared.

Denys Turner

Damaged Beauty: New Dialogue of Life

This section tangles with some difficult issues. It touches on the question of 'content' in catechesis and religious education. Jesus came to redeem, renew and fulfil our lives. His humanity is the focus of Revelation. So is all humanity and all creation. Our experiences, then, in the light of scripture and tradition, are an essential part of the content. Also, our aims in evangelising and teaching need to be clarified. Have they to do with knowledge or a transformed life, with something 'taught' or something 'caught'? Through what process is the Christian vision transmitted? How are hearts set on fire with love of God and love of the world? 'The only thing that counts for me,' wrote Pierre Teilhard de Chardin, 'is not to propagate God but to discover him. From this discovery conversion follows somewhat automatically.' How much depends on the passionate commitment of the catechist or teacher? And how much on the readiness of the student for significant change?

'It is the dialogue of life, the life of grace that we are given for others. It is life which we simultaneously possess and to which we are always on the way ... All our speech, if it is to be true speech about God, will be an act of love ...'[1]

When facing the huge and sudden changes in our amazing world that make communicating with and understanding each other so challenging, a pressing question needs to be addressed. This question is about the nature of the strategies available for transmitting these precious theological and spiritually transforming insights today.

In a postmodern world where social and cultural issues are in constant flux, where notions such as knowledge, authority and truth are undergoing an unforeseen metamorphosis, this work becomes daunting indeed. How can the courageous conversation, 'the dialogue of life', the living language of revelation, be kept alive in our new world where Christian-related words and images are, in general, no longer familiar? When a theology of nature and grace reveals a life-enhancing vision of the meaning of creation and of our lives, how is that revelation incorporated into the formation and guidance of our catechists and teachers today?

Jerome Bruner believed that 'any subject can be taught effectively in some intellectually honest form to any child at any age of development.'[2] It is important for us to remember that axiom in our efforts to present both facts and mystery. More than any other subject or topic, captivating and fascinating though they may be, the content of Christian revelation is deeply a part of mystery. Beyond a cerebral learning of the 'traditional content' of Christianity, eg scripture, doctrine or liturgy, (as ends in themselves), we realise that there is a further vital goal – the transformation of the learner. This was the goal of Jesus.

The entire enterprise is, as Jacques Maritain suggests, not so much one of gaining 'knowledge about things' as of developing 'knowledge into' the very reality and meaning of things, of humanising our knowledge; of 'guiding people in the evolving dynamism through which they shape themselves as human beings'; of bringing to realisation in people what is already God-given within their nature. To avoid squeezing the infinite soul into the limited ideas we give out, Maritain warns us to retain and respect 'the sense of each one's innermost essence and internal resources, a sort of saving and loving attention to their mysterious identity which is a hidden thing that no techniques can reach.'[3] These profound words of a great French philosopher invite us to explore some dimensions of our vital and urgent work, of our dialogue with life, in a new light.

Aim – Hope of Transformation

The General Directory for Catechesis integrates theology, spirituality and catechesis. It hopes for a profound transformation of mind and heart, by nourishing the depths of the human person in everything that he or she is (55, 57). We are dealing here with an essentially different set of aims and hopes for human fulfilment from those we are accustomed to hear about in our very competitive market. We hope that our teaching, catechising and preaching will carry a spiritual energy, a life-force, to deepen our hearers' grasp of the world, and of their own lives, and of all that is happening in them. We hope the same as Jesus hoped, that people will feel blessed and healed by the taught and caught grace of the good news. This blessing and healing of the student will be nourished and completed with a focused intensity by full participation in the sacramental life of the church.

In our schools and parishes it is a legitimate goal to aim for, that students of all ages, and from all cultures and backgrounds, will become wise enough to make more sense of the darkness and light within them, to live more abundantly, and to fall in love more deeply with God and God's world. Do we believe that our work with others is primarily to engender in them a passion for the possible, a devotion to liberating all who are unjustly oppressed, to serve the needy, to be transformed radically into courageous prophets and risk-takers?

Given the legitimacy of these aims and hopes, is there, I wonder, a skilled methodology to facilitate this transformation? In the marvellous light of a powerful and positive theology, together with a set of passionate hopes, how do we restructure and re-vision our approaches to the process of evangelising and catechising? Or do we first need to learn how to set the hearts of our catechists and teachers on fire with the vision? In *Handing on the Faith* Michael Himes quotes St Augustine's desire for enthusiasm and enjoyment on the part of the teacher and catechist. They need these graces so as to 'not only teach others – in order to instruct them; not only to delight them – in order to hold them; but also to sway them – in order to conquer and win them.' Catechising is about teaching, delighting and persuading.[4]

One cannot teach the gospel, Himes continues, which is first and foremost the story of God's love for creatures to which we should respond by loving God and our neighbour, unless one clearly and obviously loves one's students. Teaching is 'an act of love and so long as the lover is focused on the beloved and not on himself or herself, the lover cannot fail to be enthusiastic.' In recent years, when talking to pastoral ministers of the gospel, Cardinals Hume and Murphy O'Connor and Archbishops Martin (Dublin) and Williams (Canterbury) have used phrases like 'being on fire', 'being passionate', 'being totally committed to', and 'being broken and remade by the vision' so as always to be witnesses to God's free love and self-giving.

The power of passion.

Content in Catechesis

There are many questions and issues around this whole topic – too many for consideration here. Volumes have been written about the place of 'knowledge' and 'experience' in educational content. Are there, for instance, different kinds of knowledge? Is there a knowledge that could be called 'neutral' or a knowledge that is more holistically transforming? Maritain, as we have seen, distinguishes 'knowledge about' from 'knowledge into'. There is a knowledge which is 'cognitive' and there is a way of knowing that is 'affective'. Philosophers of education have discoursed about different 'forms of knowledge' and 'realms of meaning'. They have written about 'isolated learning' and 'relational knowledge'.

In his address to Catholic educators and educational leaders in the USA (April 2008) Pope Benedict emphasised the central place of a personal encounter with Jesus Christ in all their work. 'Catholic identity,' he said, 'is not to be equated simply with orthodoxy in course content ... truth means more than knowledge ...'Enlightened educators today see the teaching and learning process as sacred territory dealing with the very heart of personhood. There are phrases such as 'meaning is knowledge taken up with wisdom and interiorised with compassion' and 'wisdom is knowledge laced with love'. We have already looked at an edited extract from *A Winter Walk at Noon* by William Cowper:

> Knowledge and wisdom, far from being one,
> Have oft-times no connection. Knowledge dwells
> In heads replete with thoughts of other men;
> Wisdom in minds attentive to their own.
> Knowledge a rude unprofitable mass,
> The mere materials with which wisdom builds,
> Till smooth'd and squar'd and fitted to its place,
> Does but encumber whom it seems t'enrich.
> Knowledge is proud that he has learn'd so much;
> Wisdom is humble that he knows no more.[5]

These matters are relevant to any discussion about catechesis and religious education. The subject-matter, or 'content' in question may be merely informative or highly emotive. Scriptural study and doctrinal explanations, when considered on their own, isolated or 'neat' so to speak, are usually cerebral rather than emotive and inspiring. But when the 'cognitive content' is applied to the emotions, drives and needs of the students, then the whole enterprise takes on a different and deeper meaning. The focus shifts to the implications of Revelation (scripture and tradition) for the very lives of the students – their experiences, the quality of their life-choices, their search for inner fulfilment.

The story of catechetics in England and Wales often revolves around this issue of 'content in the curriculum'. How can 'human experience' be handled as 'content'? If the very essence of students' lives is regarded, by an incarnational theology, as the subject-matter of revelation, how can Christian educational guidelines focus on, explore, and sustain that very essence and those experiences, in such a way as to reveal to the students the sacredness of their lives? The Catholic hierarchy is always keen that objective knowledge should be passed on. Can this understandable objective go hand in hand with a more creative, poetic and experiential understanding of the faith – one that provides for the 'catching' of the imaginative vision of creation and humanity, 'the mind of Christ', as outlined in OTWTL?

There is one non-negotiable insight to hold on to in all our reflecting and debating. Karl Rahner insists that the grace of God has always been there, ahead of our preaching and teaching. These activities are not some kind of indoctrination with something from outside but 'the awakening of something within, as yet not understood but nevertheless really present. We are born into the world in the warmth of God's love which never leaves us.' That love attracts us 'like a magnet drawing pieces of iron to itself'.

The grace of God has always been there, ahead of our preaching and teaching.

A theology which perceives an integral relation between revelation and life-experience will view the educational procedure more in terms of process and development where the student is seen as unique in her personal growth and becoming. Catechists and teachers who are sensitive to such an approach will, for instance, provide opportunities for students to place their own stories in the context of the greater Story so that a new, current story is told. It is precisely around the 'skill' of entering confidently into this vision and process that much of the common anxiety and uncertainty among our catechists and teachers is found today. A renewed spiritual perception is now increasingly essential for bringing about a deepening understanding of the aims and work of Catholic education.

First there is the provision of occasions for students to reflect on what they have seen, done, learnt, suffered and enjoyed. There is the drawing out from them how they reacted to those experiences, the meaning they gave to them, the emotions they felt. Then there is the reviewing and consideration of this exercise in the light of Christian revelation about the deeper personal and universal significance of all life's experiences. Such sharing contributes to self-knowledge, self-transcendence, personal freedom and true human growth, which are part of the desired outcome of Christian education.

Because some obvious questions arise here, much attention will be devoted to this process in the following pages. What part of this holy work can be achieved in the more formal setting of structured sessions? How can people, in any setting, be brought to the limits of their own creativity and imagination, to the 'moment of disclosure'? How can they, in the light of incarnation, be enabled to de-code, to interpret their own mystery? For this work to be effective, how important is it for the student to be continually participating in the life and liturgies of the parish and of the wider church communities?

Educationalist and philosopher John Dewey held that all education is about self-realisation as well as intellectual development. The content of the curriculum, he wrote, should assist in 'freeing the life-process for its own most adequate fulfilment'; it must be restored to the experience from which it has grown. 'It needs to be turned over, translated into the immediate and personal experience within which it has its origin and significance.'

Dewey's comments are helpful in working towards a solution to a continually-debated question among religious educationalists regarding their work with students. It is a question about the place of sheer religious knowledge in current approaches to RCIA programmes, school syllabuses, first sacrament sessions, and adult formation guidelines. It is, as we have observed, probably the most commonly debated and emotive issue facing catechetics and RE today.

What helps to clarify the understandable anxiety around this question (of the place of knowledge) is to assert that nothing of value in the deposit of faith, in the accumulated teachings of the *magisterium*, is neglected or dismissed. The essential, suggested shift in the identification of the 'content' is this: instead of being presented, learnt, examined, as the full subject-matter in its own right, as it often used to be (and often still is), in this suggested approach, the body of knowledge, doctrines, teachings, etc is still an essential dimension of the whole equation of catechesis and RE, but with a wonderfully more dynamic intention.

Some clarification is provided by Dr Dermot Lane, former Director of Studies at Mater Dei Institute for Education in Dublin. He holds that the task of theology and its transmission is to keep the human being alive and active in the divine-human exchange. If the reality of the loving relationship between God and God's people is seen simply as something that can be summed up in a body of truths, then the emphasis in church education will be one of safeguarding the deposit of faith. This will lead inevitably to an excessive concern with the defence of a verbal orthodoxy at the expense of a living active faith among the people of God. Such defence will fall on the deaf ears of contemporary students in a postmodern world during a communications revolution where the medium is the message.

But if the loving relationship between God and humanity is seen as something that goes beyond a body of truths into the deeper realms of the interpersonal, the experiential and the historical, then the concern of Christian education will be to express that relationship in a language, and through a catechetical method, that is in touch with people's present, personal experience of God in their lives.

Head and Heart together

A central concern of ours in working with the implications of OTWTL in this current project, is to ensure that none of the traditional contents of the Catholic faith is overlooked in our presentation of a renewed Christian vision. For instance, the recovery of a theology of nature and grace is never achieved at the expense of any orthodox teachings regarding original sin and a theology of redemption.

The *Begin with the Heart* project embraces all the central teachings and practices of our tradition, seeing them as necessary nourishment and guidelines along the journey of each soul and each community, keeping the vision of God alive for us on the way to life. It is important to emphasise that there is no down-playing of formal teaching and learning in our efforts to grasp and interiorise the richness of the understanding of sacramentality.

Part Three endeavours to clarify the fact that in the overall 'content' of our 'handing on' of the faith, there is no necessary conflict between the place of human experience and the place of the doctrines of our tradition. The 'content' of our lived lives on the one hand, and that of scripture and tradition on the other, can never be over-against each other, as though they were in competition for pride of place. Like nature and grace, they go, and grow, together. Revealed truth cannot work against itself.

It follows that the truths of the church and her essential beliefs, the familiar 'four pillars of Catholic faith' as found in the *Catechism of the Catholic Church* and in the *Compendium of the Catechism* – are all at the heart of any real renewal of our catechetical work. What is being clarified in the project is the overall shape and coherence of our approach, the manner in which all our teaching and learning patiently works towards the final goal of a transformed life and vision, personally and universally, through union with God. There is an exciting time ahead for all those concerned with evangelisation, catechesis and religious

It is important to emphasise that there is no down-playing of formal teaching and learning in our efforts to grasp and interiorise the richness of the understanding of sacramentality.

education in the creating of a dynamic structuring and sequencing of the 'content' of our guidelines so as to be always true to the sacramental vision, the mind of Christ.

It is worth emphasising that the necessary knowing and memorising of the basic beliefs of the Catholic faith are never an end in themselves. While that fact is always asserted by our enlightened leaders, it is not always clearly understood by the enlightened followers. In *Things Hidden,* Franciscan Richard Rohr's classic on scripture and spirituality, he writes: 'Nothing in this world is an end in itself – including church, pastors, priests, bishops, popes, laws, Bible – nothing. Only God is an end; everything else is a means. Only God can save us.'[6] The only true purpose of evangelising, catechising and a more formal teaching is the transformation of each person and of each community into the new creation of unity and intimacy with the heart of God. It is to reveal and to release the graced, abundant life that we all already carry within us.

In *Fit for Mission? Schools* Bishop Patrick O'Donoghue writes about the vital relationship between the content of faith and the reality of personal experience. 'Interpreting and illuminating personal life with the truths and data of faith should be the overall focus of teaching the faith in schools'.[7] He quotes Cardinal Schönborn who wrote that catechesis opens up space for new experiences beyond our normal ones.

It does this by exploring, purifying, intensifying and celebrating our everyday experiences.

How we understand this part of the mystery is a key issue. It is not so much a question about which source of revelation (human experience or scripture and tradition) gets the lion's share of attention. The whole focus of our endeavour in our pastoral ministries lies in how precisely we see these two as interdependent. That is the wise skill, the Spirit's gift of understanding, that all teachers and preachers need to acquire. That is what lies at the heart of these pages.

The accurate and balanced grasp of the meaning of revelation, of the sacramental vision at the heart of incarnation, provides the context and contours of our approaches to any kind of faith-mission. How we perceive the incarnational nature of redemption, and how we are personally transformed by it, will radically colour our motives and methods in sharing the good news with our students. Getting the vision clear, and then the tactics for realising it, is a crucial challenge for those responsible for the faith development of young and old today, for the very future of the church. The catechist works towards the faith-horizon that sees the mystery of the incarnation, and all the traditional dimensions of the church, as revealing the hand and heart of God already and always at work in the daily life of each person, and of the universe itself.

Michael Himes refers to Cardinal Newman's *An Essay in Aid of a Grammar of Assent* where he distinguishes between 'notional assent' (the acceptance of the truth of an inference) and 'real assent' (the acceptance of an experience). Himes writes, 'Communicating faith is not primarily a matter of supplying propositions and information (although that is part of faith) but rather evoking and naming experiences. The teacher of faith should help his hearers examine their experience and offer categories to them for understanding that experience. Teaching faith is, in a sense, offering people a hermeneutic for interpreting what they experience within and around themselves so that disparate parts of their experience begin to connect and emerge as a meaningful whole.'[8]

Naming the place of grace.

Love before Knowledge

That is why the vital elements of scripture and tradition are more than signposts to be known. They are experiences to be entered into. Anthony de Mello is remembered for his stories. One of them is about going on a journey. 'Imagine you wish to go to York. So you travel to York. At a certain point in your journey you come to a large sign which says *York*. You do not stop at this sign. No, you go beyond the sign and journey to your destination.'

Too often we stop and stay at the sign. Many catechisms are made up of wonderful signs and directions. But they are not the experience of faith. They speak of salvation, sin, grace, freedom and many other gifts of God that are so important for our lives. Too often we do not go beyond the knowing and learning of these potentially life-changing facts and promises. We do not ask what they mean in practice. We are not told how to cash this revealed treasure into the currency of a life lived. We are not drawn into the adventure of exploring the personal and communal transformation that union with God makes in our lives.

> This exploration cannot be achieved in our heads alone. It is not enough to know the central beliefs of our faith; it is not enough to teach and proclaim them. They must be embodied and lived out in every dimension of our lives, and not only as individuals but as communities as well. In the incarnate mystery of our faith, the teachings on the one hand, and our ordinary lives on the other, are not separate realities. Nor is it enough to say that they are linked. They are essential to each other. For the Christian they only come to true life when they work and play off each

other, finding their full expression in each other. This vision of the unique enfleshing of divine revelation is the work of the Catholic imagination.

In *The Menu is not the Meal*[9] Seamus O'Connell, Professor of Sacred Scripture at St Patrick's College, Maynooth, refers to people in a restaurant who refuse to put down the menu! For want of better guidance and catechesis, we stay staring at the guidelines, the lists to be known and remembered, and too often we do not actually taste the food that renews our life. He quotes St Bernard of Clairvaux: 'May the Word who in the beginning was with God, become flesh of my flesh … Let it not be a written and mute word, but one incarnate and living, that is to say, not a word scratched by dumb signs on dead skins, but one in human form truly traced by the working of the Holy Spirit' (Homily IV,11)

Known faith must become lived faith.

Many of our syllabuses are like holy menus compiled of essential teachings and formulations. But *known* faith must become *lived* faith. Remembering the items on the menu is one thing: being nourished by the actual food is another. We must become the truths we learn. As food is useless until it is consumed thus transforming our bodies, so all the beliefs in the world will not nourish and save our souls unless, and until, they are welcomed by heart, mind and spirit. O'Connell quotes from Vatican II's *Dei Verbum*: 'The Church … receives and offers to the faithful the bread of life from the table both of God's word and of Christ's body.'

Referring to the work of catechesis, another contributor writes: 'We are so worried by the task of "passing on the faith", and so concerned to "leave nothing out", that we have often dropped that beautiful burden – disguised it, concealed it, lost it – and many children and adults now never receive it.' The 'beautiful burden' he refers to is the primacy of communicating love in all our educational ministries, the experience of God's presence at all times. This, he writes, is 'the beautiful truth, the summit of the hierarchy of truths, the primary obligation of all Christian teaching and preaching.'[10]

Re-setting the Compass

The reason for today's situation of ambiguity and uncertainty about the content and aim of catechesis may arise from this; maybe those who inspired and created some of our current syllabuses in the aftermath of Vatican II's theology had a clear and incarnational vision of the goals and methods of catechesis and formation. They placed human experiences and created realities first in the process of each presentation because, as we have tried to show, in the light of the incarnation, this is where the journey begins – and ends. The vision behind this way of working may have initially been misunderstood, due, perhaps, to inadequate preparation of teachers and catechists for it, and then too often lost, in recent decades, in the subsequent implementation of such syllabuses across the country.

Critics of contemporary programmes say that they are reminiscent of the old-fashioned catechism-like programmes, but with a superficially-related event or experience at the beginning. That is why teachers – and many of our church leaders – are uneasy with what seems an unnecessarily complicated way of doing things. They are anxious about the proportion of time and attention given to the 'human experience segment' of the syllabus units at the expense of the place of knowledge of divine revelation.

> But this incarnational principle in catechesis and religious education, of moving from life to revelation and back again so as to transform our lives, makes total good sense when seen in the context of the basic relationship between nature and grace in the economy of salvation.

That is the vital vision that changes everything in the work of evangelising and catechising. The catechetical compass needs to be reset to true North. An attempt is made to do this in the next section.

Once this central relationship is understood and accepted, then the necessary place of the life-topic and experience-theme becomes clear. Until the reasons for this vision and these tactics are understood, there will be persistent calls for a catechesis and for religious education schemes based on teachings, knowledge and church attendance alone rather than on a passionate heart and a transformed life, as well.

Christ at the Centre[11] offers a clear, coherent summary of why the church provides Catholic schools. Many excellent reasons are given for this provision, emphasising the unique service to personal integrity, to Christian values in the family, in the parish community, contributing to the common good of society. Christ will always be at the centre in a Catholic education that offers a spiritual, systematic and cultural education for young people in today's world.

Begin with the Heart endeavours to make all these aims and aspirations achievable by emphasising a basic Catholic sacramental vision which ensures that Christ is, indeed, always cherished at the centre of our educational work in parish catechesis, school education and liturgical preaching. This section is an attempt to 'unpack', to explicate and to inculcate what we mean by gospel values and Catholic ethos in the light of a sacramental traditional.

Information and Transformation

'Information and personal intimacy,' writes Fr Roderick Strange, 'instead of being seen as companions, have sometimes been cast as antagonists. There have been those who insisted on the importance of content, and those who have championed process ... The weakness in both viewpoints, when taken to extremes, has been to assume that, if one element were secure, the other would follow automatically.'[12] The writer goes on to emphasise the necessary place of both approaches. But the approaches are not equal. The deeper and more abiding is the winning over of the heart. Necessary and appropriate as it may be, unless knowledge alone is transcended, the person of Jesus will not capture our imagination or our hearts. Wallace Stephens writes:

> We come
> To knowledge when we come to life.
> Yet always there is another life,
> A life beyond this present knowing,
> A life lighter than this present splendour ...
> Not an attainment of the will
> But something illogically received,
> A divination, a letting down
> From loftiness, misgivings dazzlingly
> Resolved in dazzling discovery.[13]

Take the mother who sees it as her calling to instil a deep love of music in her children. She will enter into all the details of the history and background of music with them, encouraging them to learn a hundred pieces of information, facilitating their endless hours of practice, leaving nothing to chance, making sure that there are no flaws in their techniques, no holes in their knowledge about their shared interest. But most important, and through it all it is the mother's passion for her subject that will drive and draw everything. It is her deep love for both her subject and her children that will colour the cold facts and routine, so that those children will be on fire, despite the hard graft of learning, with the same passion as their mother. In the end, it is because her own heart is alive with the joy and pleasure that music brings into her life that, unerringly, those young hearts will be transformed too.

But how can teachers and catechists hold that loving and patient attention first in their own hearts? How do they create a readiness for the sacramental vision in their students? For a start they have a theology of nature and grace which emphasises the sacredness of all our human experiences. According to the authors of OTWTL, 'It is a theology that makes explicit "the eternity in the heart" of every human person which is constantly seeking expression and form.'[14] We are here in the land of sacramental imagination.

How is vision transmitted? And how do hearts catch fire? How, for instance, in disciplines such as music, poetry or painting, do teachers instil a passion in their students? Or is it all about creating the conditions for glimpses and unpredictable 'moments' to happen? Is the catechist's work to provide a readiness within their listeners for identifying the daily epiphanies that fill their lives?; to facilitate, like a midwife, the emergence of what is already waiting within them to be born? As Bruner believed, 'Discovery, like surprise, favours the prepared mind.' There is a great deal of wisdom in such thinking. We often have to wait a long time for change to happen!

How do hearts catch fire?

These are some of the challenges facing the teacher and catechist as they present and balance their material for the students. On the one hand there are the means of salvation such as church doctrines, scripture, sacraments and, on the other, the experience of that salvation, that union with God in Christ, in the here and now. Clarity in this matter will have much impact on the vision and tactics deployed in the educational work and in the way it is received by the students. *En passant*, this confusion can be lessened by making a distinction between belief in God, on the one hand, and belief in the church on the other.

The eminent Catholic theologian Cardinal Walter Kasper holds that 'The church and all that accompanies it, particularly the sacraments and offices, are believed in a different way from our belief in God, who acts in Jesus Christ through the Holy Spirit for salvation. It is to God alone that faith is directly related, and it is God who forms the real content of that faith. The church, together with its sacraments and offices, is only a means of salvation, and faith is related to it to the extent that it mediates salvation and makes it present ... The means of salvation have to be seen as ways in which salvation is mediated, and if they are no longer satisfactorily performing this function, they should be criticised.'[15]

Following on from an incarnational understanding of the humanity of Jesus, a theology of nature and grace, as elegantly and forcefully presented in OTWTL, sees human experience as the locus and focus of divine revelation. What is highlighted here is that the lives we live, and the human emotions we undergo, are at the heart of the 'content' of the guidelines and syllabuses. The essential place of the information, knowledge and teachings of the faith is assured because it is only in the light of what they offer that the human experiences being explored can be shown to be filled with God's grace, to be God's chosen home, to be the dwelling-place of the in-dwelling Blessed Trinity.

The anxieties of catechists.

There are more questions around these issues. Do our catechists and teachers, for instance, feel comfortable and competent in seeing their work along these profound but simple lines of unfolding? Do they feel theologically adequate and personally convinced about the truths implied in this way of evangelising and catechising? How much of what we hope for, as a promising new design, is possible in light of the official emphases on attainment targets, success lists, and assessment levels in a highly competitive market? Where schools are concerned, do teachers think that the classic distinction between 'objective' RE in school and 'subjective' catechesis in the parish should be restored?

Many people correctly believe that students should be able to articulate clearly the faith that is within them, to give a satisfactory account of their reasons for believing the life-transforming revelation of Jesus. This point is well made in a letter to *The Tablet*. 'As a parent I see my children growing into young people exposed to popular youth culture in which materialism, relativism and individualism are major forces ... In this context I want our children to have words to describe their faith, which will face all sorts of threats and relativising pressures as they grow up in a post-modern world.'

Is there too much expected of the RE teacher, the catechist and chaplain in all of this discussion; a presumption of unusual talents and graces on their part? Is there a danger of forgetting the art of the possible? The responsibility shifts and lightens a little when we realise that such a legitimate expectation is meant to be shared by all who work in Catholic education.

> There is a realisation that is gradually and urgently becoming more clear at this time in the life of the church – it is the whole school staff, and all who participate in the wider school and parish communities, who carry the responsibility for creating the radically different ministry that lies at the heart of Catholic education. This is another way of saying that until the pressing need for a vibrant vision and well-planned strategy for educational and catechetical renewal is met, then our current anxieties will continue.

Because we are dealing with divine/human mystery here, there will never be one perfect approach. Maybe the whole enterprise of a liberating transmission of a vibrant sacramental vision is a mixture of many 'contents', 'presences' and processes – i) the appropriate subject-matter or formal knowledge, ii) the central place of the 'raw-material' of actual experience to be interpreted, iii) the hope of preparing a readiness for a deeper, transforming understanding of life in the future, iv) the thorough, personal conviction of the catechist or teacher about the wonder and beauty of insights they endeavour to instil and v) the powerful influence of the wider Christian community – e.g. family and parish – in the formation of the young soul. (See 'Courageous Conversations' at end of this Part.)

> Through the careful study of the sources of revelation such as the scriptures, doctrine and liturgy, the Spirit-filled catechist reveals to the students the deeper significance of their experiences in the world, in such a way as to purify and intensify the quality of their lives. In prayer, sacrament and abundant living, then, they praise and thank the God of Life.

'I was born a man,' said Abraham Heschel, 'and now my task is to become human.' The real content of our endeavours is not only the knowledge, facts, information about the faith – in themselves; it is about how they reveal God's secret about life itself. And not life in an abstract, philosophical sense, but life as it is lived and experienced by child and adult alike, seeking and discovering, right here and right now, an abundance and a transformation in their deepest core, through an intimacy with Jesus, the Son of God, the Human One.

The Spiritual Student

Once the whole enterprise of evangelising, forming, educating and preaching is underpinned by a theology of nature and grace, then a great deal of shifting from our former categories, assumptions and habits has to happen. Everything is affected; everything assumes a renewed meaning. For instance, the way we perceive those students that we serve is significantly changed. They are honoured as human beings made in God's image with a divine hunger and thirst for a spiritual and holistic flowering, the seeds of which are already waiting within them. This sacred space of their (and our) humanity is the only threshold where a true meeting of minds and hearts can happen. And this human threshold will usually have much pain around it.

All students carry a memory in their hearts. They have come from God and are fashioned in the divine image. The longing they carry for completion is God's own longing inscribed on their souls from the beginning. Their listening ear, their readiness for understanding, their openness for transformation, their waiting for the Word, is already God's loving gift in their souls. The teacher's role is to set this yearning free; to unblock all that is stifling the expansion of the very nature of their true being.

As explored in Part Two, central to a theology of nature and grace is the revelation, (first in the hypostatic union in Christ), that God has placed in each student's essence a graced capacity, a readiness and aptitude for hearing the Word, for welcoming the Spirit, for intimacy with God. The role of the catechist, of the priest, of the teacher, is to nurture and coax into fullness what is already within. The Buddhists hold that 'unblocked the eyes will see, unwaxed the ears will hear, unburdened the heart will love.' The task is to protect the fragile flame that waits within, ready for fanning into greater light and life.

The role of the catechist, of the priest, of the teacher, is to nurture and coax into fullness what is already within.

It is the time of the 17th century Great Plague in Eyam, Derbyshire. The small community heroically decided to close off all communication with the outside world so as to contain the deadly disease within their village. Most of them died horrible deaths. Towards the end of those fateful months, Mrs Montpellion, the vicar's wife, despite her illness, whispers these words of hope to her despairing helper. Anna, having lost her husband and two small boys, felt the very life had drained out of her. 'I wonder if you know how much you have changed. It is the one good, perhaps, to have come out of this terrible year. Oh, the spark was clear in you when you first came to us – but you covered your light as if you were afraid of what would happen if anyone saw it. You were like a flame blown by the wind until it almost went out. All I had to do was to put the glass around you. And now, oh how you shine!'[16]

Our best teachers and catechists are well aware of the intrinsic connection between education and imagination. For many, however, it is a goal too far. Yet this is the task of the educator – to protect the unique originality of each student, 'to put the glass around her'. It surely saddens the Spirit when bad teaching serves only to stunt and wither the essential potential of every learner for transformation of consciousness.

> To block the flow of creativity in the human heart is a spiritual crime because then the flow of grace is blocked too. There can be no justification, no matter what or who its source may be, for any approach to Christian education in any of its many forms, that has as its primary aim anything other than the flowering of the divine imagination in every student. Here is a fine challenge for the curriculum-planners, programme-makers and preachers to ensure that this central concern is always honoured.

Put another way, our curriculum and guidelines must begin and end with this central recognition of the intrinsic sacredness of all the student's experiences and endeavours, however limited or 'merely human' they may appear to be. Students are seekers of God to the extent that they explore, play, love, create, imagine and attempt to achieve self-discovery. As Christian educators our concern is to assist students in developing that dimension of awareness of their relationships with themselves, with others and the world itself. Those experiences, as we have been at pains to emphasise, are the raw material of their experience of the Blessed Trinity already within them. The task is to bring the pre-reflexive (unexamined) dimension of the student's life to self-consciousness in the light of Christ, the paradigm of full human transcendence.

To take one example. The most fundamental area of energy, emotion and potential disclosure for students is in the world of the relational. The quality of their relationships is the most formative and revelatory experience and influence in their lives. The Christian educator will enter into a nurturing alliance with the student, a kind of *anam-chara*, as Jesus was, with all those who wished to walk and talk with him. He endeavoured to educate the emotions. For our students, this education will emphasise the power of our love and friendship to bring others to their full beauty. It will also include the capacity of a relationship to cause great damage.

Given the pressure on our agents of education to complete the curriculum, to ensure top exam results, where is the time to offer careful guidance regarding healthy boundaries, mutual respect, a spirit of generosity and service, emotional intelligence and literacy – all those graced and hard-won habits of the soul that protect the incarnate love of God in very fragile human beings? The heart, too, needs educating. Without due education it goes out of kilter; it cannot cope because it cannot express itself. The mind takes over and rules the show. Without an animating, educated heart, the intellect appears superior, and we give too much attention and value to it.

> The 'mindful heart' will see and hear the heartbeat of God in all the heartbeats that fill and lift the world every day. Especially in the heartbeats of our students – our spiritual students whose human longing for the abundant life reflects God's own desire for union with us.

In the next section we continue the crucial debate about areas of content in catechesis and religious education. This issue is never far away. When we can share, in a Christian spirit, our differing views about what is most necessary, orthodox and effective in this holy work, all of us will be enriched – especially the lives of our students, young and old.

Summary

Much debate centres on what is meant by the term 'content' in our catechesis and preaching. There is a need for clarity about our understanding of 'knowledge', of 'human experience' and of how they interconnect and complete each other.

The real content of our endeavours is not only a mastery of the knowledge, facts and information about the faith, in themselves – it is about how they reveal God's secret about the love and meaning in each student's life-experiences, and in the world itself. *The General Directory of Catechesis* hopes for a profound transformation of mind and heart by nourishing the depths of the human person in everything that he or she is.

Is it realistic to expect teachers and catechists to have a passion, a charisma, for their faith and for spreading its vision? And are they confident in their understanding of the theology that underpins the vision?

The source of that vision, of the teacher's inspiration, of the whole transforming process, is the humanity of Jesus.

All essential Catholic teaching finds its rightful place in a catechesis that nurtures the sacramental imagination based on a theology of nature and grace.

Faithfulness to the Catholic sacramental vision in our educational endeavours will always ensure that Christ is at the centre.

Head and heart combine in the total transformation of the human person. But love will always come before knowledge.

'All our speech (catechising, preaching) if it is to be true speech about God, will be an act of love ...' (OTWTL)

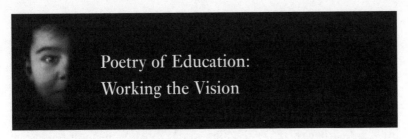

Poetry of Education:
Working the Vision

The design for 'working the vision' outlined here, follows an underlying threefold dialectic in all our catechetical, pedagogical and, indeed, homiletic strategies. An incarnational approach to catechesis, RE and all pastoral ministry takes its starting-point from the real lived experience of the student. Its end-point then, in the light of what Jesus did and who he was, is that same human experience, but now understood and experienced as transformed. This is where the call to mission is heard, and responded to, in a new and powerful way.

Ludwig Wittgenstein observed that it is experience, especially the experience of love, that makes the resurrection credible. Writer Donal Dorr says that the theology that interests him is that which reflects on spiritual experience – his own and that of his travelling companions. Sebastian Moore writes about theology in terms of his personal story known to God alone 'of my dialogue with ultimate reality'. This story is awakened by the story of Jesus. We are talking then about a certain kind of theology - and, it follows, a certain way of teaching it.[17]

In the light of what Professor Terence McLaughlin calls the 'coherent, striking theological vision' of OTWTL, it seems reasonable enough to assume, for the moment, that an experience-based approach to teaching and learning would be an appropriate 'vehicle of transmission' for such a vision. To some extent, at least in the opening units of any given subject-matter, most of our current syllabuses, guidelines and schemes of work adopt this approach. Their beginnings are firmly based on the events, experiences and realities of the lives of the students, young and old.

Whereas formerly, the information and knowledge that all Catholics were required to know were contained in a catechism or similar textbook, today, almost all the officially recommended syllabuses start off with experience-based life-themes and topics with which the students are familiar. We need, however, to understand why this is so, and to explore further about its efficacy, because, as we have already briefly discussed, something often goes askew in the course of the process. The promising beginning is not always carried through.

Simplifying the Process

In broad outline there is a teaching strategy that seems to fit the vision of a theology of nature and grace. Arising from the basic 'nature/grace' movement within such a theology, it seems appropriate to have three fundamental phases in an appropriate educational pattern. The first phase looks at aspects of personal experience, creation and the human condition (nature). After the creative exploring by the students of these aspects and experiences, the transforming light shed on them by the birth and Passover of Jesus Christ (grace) is then revealed. This is the good news that changes everything. The third phase is where the new awareness of this deeper love and meaning at the heart of students' lives and loves (the new creation) is constantly purified, persevered in, delighted in, and celebrated in all kinds of ways. This is the awareness that motivates and empowers the students with a sense of mission and service to the world. In a sense, there is an echo of our understanding of the baptismal catechumenate in this general groundplan.

Three phases of Christian education.

Put another way, this design suggests an underlying threefold dialectic in all our catechetical, pedagogical and, indeed, homiletic strategies. An incarnational approach to catechesis, school-RE and all pastoral ministry takes its starting-point from the real lived experience of the student. Its end-point then, in the light of what Jesus did and who he was, is that same human experience, but now transformed. The student is growing into a profound understanding of her newly-enhanced, newly-deepened, now 'Christened' humanity – a humanity with immense possibilities for love, growth, and ever-deeper meaning. Between these two lived realities – the students' ordinary, pre-reflexive life-experience and its deepest, ultimate meaning – lies the essential mediating traditions and practices of scripture, doctrine, the liturgy, and the life-witness of Christian saints and scholars. (See fig. A)

In our parishes and schools the work of catechesis and teaching is structured into a scheme or set of guidelines where some kind of 'life-theme' will usually be found. When appropriately integrated, it is a worthy companion for a theology of nature and grace. They are both (the theology and the educational approach) committed to the examination and the enhancement of life-experience and of humanity itself. But they do

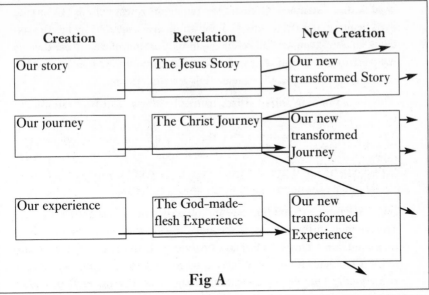

Fig A

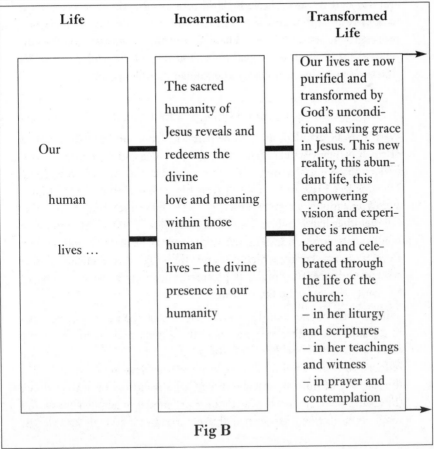

Fig B

need to understand each other. Otherwise, as Professor John Hull wrote in 'Theology of Life-Themes' there will be innumerable 'category mistakes' in the 'dualistic follow-through' of this approach, where themes 'go wild' and 'go to seed', where the precise and unique theology of the sacred *vis-à-vis* the secular is generally misunderstood.

This is happening today. Teachers confess to a confusion about the theory and practice of many current catechetical outlines and content. They are a bit at sea about how the 'life part' and the 'religious part' relate to each other. When that vital and intrinsic interconnection between nature and grace is unclear, or missed out completely, then the whole inner cohesion of such programmes collapses.

Some syllabuses are ambiguous and inconsistent in how they set out to achieve their ultimate aims. It was noted earlier that while the introductory guidelines may be clear and in line with the main thrust of the OTWTL suggestions for effective teaching and learning, the actual subsequent structure, sequence and nature of the material provided seem to end up at odds with those promising aims. The basic inner coherence too often gets lost together with the relevance of the whole process to the students' lives. That is one of the main reason for the current anxiety around this urgent issue. The neglected insights of *On The Threshold* provide great clarity and guidance at this point.

On The Threshold

What is to be avoided, on the one hand, in school and parish, is a view of the life-theme which holds human experience and contemporary situations to be initial sources of interest for the students, whereby life is linked with Christianity in a well-intentioned but perfunctory fashion – an *extrinsic* model which reverts back to the formal teaching of the past. On the other hand, to be avoided also, is a view of the life-theme which holds the exploration into human experience to be in itself, and without Revelation, an activity which discloses the religious dimension of that same experience. But, much as postmodernism might wish it to be so, humanity can never be the measure of itself.

Humanity can never be the measure of itself.

What mostly happens in the overall teaching of the themes in our current guidelines is that at some stage the vitality and creativity of the explorations into the heart of the students' life ceases, or they are reduced to being a point of entry into the 'transmission of knowledge', the learning of information about the Catholic faith. This way of doing things has many similarities with a former model, when catechesis and religious education were seen as the imparting of a body of knowledge, a 'deposit of faith', where the students assimilate the facts about the main contents of faith – usually a grasp of scripture, of selected doctrines and of reasons for participation in the church's liturgy. In a sense, they were often assimilated for their own sake, as necessary supportive material for apologetics and healthy argument, but not primarily for the powerful, personal and transforming effect they would have on the quality of the students' lives.

As OTWTL keeps reminding us, a return to the insights of the Second Vatican Council brings a much-needed focus. 'We must be aware of, and understand, the aspirations, the yearnings, and the often dramatic features of the world we live in. At all times the church carries the responsibilities of reading the signs of the times, and of interpreting them in the light of the gospel, if it is to carry out its task.'[18] What is clarified here is the intrinsic relationship between the way things are and the way things can be; the reality of the world and the reality of salvation; the signs of the times and the light of the gospel, the human story and the story of God.

'Whatever we may think of today's society, its good points and its bad points, we are called by God to examine it. This is not an optional extra. The wonder and the grief, the uncertainties and the yearnings of those who come and stand on the threshold of the church with us are our joys and sorrows too.'[19] This shared humanity is the common ground, the threshold or doorstep, on which both catechised and catechist stand so that the two-way streams of grace may flow. It is, in fact, given the truth of the incarnation, the only threshold for the good news to be uttered and heard, for the human/divine encounter to take place.

> 'God is at work in people's lives. They come to us with life experience in which God has already been active whether they have recognised this or not.'[20]

This observation from *On the Threshold* is, of course, the inevitable consequence of a theology of nature and grace. The whole enterprise of sharing the faith on the journey of life is based on this understanding of revelation. 'The sense of the sacred and the search for something to make sense of life is very strong in our society. People may not explicitly call this a search for God but it is an open door for the church's message. This search for God, or however the search is expressed, is a desire for meaning and depth in what is often experienced as an increasingly shallow, brittle society. However, rarely do people equate this as having anything to do with "church".'[21]

So all-pervasive still is the deadly virus of dualism, where the essential truth of the incarnation is denied, that we persist in regarding these human yearnings for, and intimations of, a higher love as 'merely' human, devoid of the divine. 'Churchless', or 'religionless', much of our society may be, but 'Godless' or 'unspiritual' it is not. It is extraordinary that so many Christians use these epithets for our world today. Such well-meaning but negative descriptions do not spring from a theology of nature and grace.

Intrinsic Model

To repeat, the use of human experience in a renewed, life-theme design is not meant to be a way of capturing the students' interest before bringing in the explicitly 'religious knowledge' dimension, nor is the human experience content meant to be the self-contained locus of 'implicitly' religious values, carrying *within itself alone* the revelation of their own meaning. Rather an *intrinsic* model seeks to maintain, within the life-theme design, the integrity of both the 'sacred' and the 'secular' elements of experience. This has to be so because the experience explored in the life-theme constitutes that basic condition for Christian revelation which can be mediated *only in terms* of that human experience.

> A theology of nature and grace insists on the intrinsic relation between the life experience of the students and the specifically revelatory dimension of Christianity. The key to the clarifying and focusing of that intrinsic relationship is the sacramental vision.

The authors of OTWTL point out that grace is an integral part of human nature, pushing it towards completion in God. This theology gives a basis for a Christ-centred humanism. 'Contemporary culture claims humanity as its own and makes it the measure of itself. The Second Vatican Council proposes an understanding of humanity which accepts what contemporary culture has to say about it in part, but completes it with the rich vision of humanity and its history transformed in Christ so that human beings and their culture may be seen as sacramental, finite realities which display the being of God because God has made his dwelling in them.'[22]

A theology of nature and grace in fact, far from denigrating the beauty, values and worth-whileness of created things and human experiences, is dedicated to protecting, pruning and nurturing into growth and full self-expression that very beauty, those very values, their essentially divine potential for which they were created by God in the first place.

To sum up, that is why, in this renewed life-theme design, the initial exploration into human experience as we have it today in schools and parishes across the country, is not to be regarded as a kind of preamble to some central religious input, but is, *in itself* (and only in itself, in *this* time, place and person) the necessary locus that is refined and purified, enlightened and humanised, saved and perfected, by the new design of love as revealed in Christ. As put so pithily by the authors of OTWTL, 'Christ is the completion of the human project.' This visionary approach will view the educational procedure more in terms of process and development in a dialectical curriculum model. The student is seen as unique in her personal growth and becoming, and all the factors involved in this process are recognised and acknowledged as intrinsic to her understanding, acceptance and experience of a personal, dynamic and divine revelation. (See Fig B, p 111)

> In other words, what is important to remember is that however we organise our material – the basic constituents of our faith, usually seen as the scriptures, dogmas and doctrines, participation in the sacramental life of the church, and the witness of the saints – they must be handled in such a manner as to clarify, purify, celebrate and reveal a human nature in which the most intimate presence of God, the indwelling Trinity, is already dwelling forever at home.

'Experience', then, should not be considered as an additional, preliminary 'content-area' for catechesis or RE. Rather it constitutes the existential condition for God's saving action to be revealed in every detail of our lives. The continually graced character of human experience, with all its suffering, joys, encounters and disappointments, is essentially revelatory; for in it resides the capacity for transcendence, for the discovery of love and meaning at its very heart. The task and privilege of the teacher and catechist is to bring the image of God, already incontrovertibly secure at the core of each human's life and of the life of the world, to the edge of their experience – ever closer, as St Paul reminds us, to the shining likeness of God, through the medium of knowledge and formation in the graced beliefs, rituals and daily lives of the Christian community. This is where we find the Catholic imagination, the sacramental vision, at its best.

Put another way, any 'distinction' does not lie between 'mere' human experience, (whether of one's own deeper reality or that of the world) on the one hand and 'divine revelation' on the other, as though they were both essentially unconnected. It lies in the dimension of awareness relating to one and the same reality; namely, that as a matter of faith, all life, all experience, all knowledge is encompassed by the Spirit of Christ

– from the moment of creation when the opening Word of dialogue was first uttered, through the dawn of the Resurrection, when the conversation was definitively taken up and fulfilled.

Because a theology of nature and grace is often called upon to defend itself against the (false) accusation of taking the reality of sin too lightly, this may be the moment to emphasise here that the reality of original sin is all-pervasive. (It is all pervasive but never all-victorious.) This whole educational approach centres on the constant need for the particular and general experiences of the students to be critiqued, adjusted and redeemed in the light of revelation. The lives we live must be purified and saved so as to body forth what they already essentially are.

While God is hidden in the most ordinary of things, experiences, creation, there is always something that prevents us from recognising that presence. There is an innate myopia that misses the subtle light. We are so easily allured by false gods and goddesses. We are congenitally addicted to our flawed selves, blind to the injustice and fear all around us. That is why the saving dimension of healing and purifying must always be central to whatever way we teach or preach. Jesus came, not to specialise in religion and sin, but simply to dry up tears, to gladden hearts, to heal minds and bodies and finally, by convincing people of how accepted they were, to set them free. We serve people, as Jesus did, by continually liberating them, young and old, from all within and around them that persistently and ubiquitously oppresses and diminishes them. When that sense of service comes first, with all its dying, the rest follows, with all its rising.

'We may say,' observes W .H. Vanstone, 'that Christ, the Incarnate Word, discloses to us, at the climax of his life, what word it was that God spoke when he commanded and creation happened. It was no light or idle word but the Word of love.'[23] Towards the end of OTWTL the authors point out that 'in his seminal primer for all Christian religious education, catechesis and formation, St Augustine reminds us that this dialogue of life is not about us but about God – the God who is love. All our speech, if it is true speech about this God, will be an act of love.'

Theology and Themes

'The first and most obvious problem,' writes Jerome Bruner, 'is how to construct curricula that can be taught by ordinary teachers to ordinary pupils and that at the same time reflect clearly the basic underlying principles of various fields of enquiry.'[24]

In addressing similar issues within the world of Christian evangelisation

and formation, there are certain theological underpinnings that the catechist or teacher needs to keep always in mind. The new consciousness
that has transformed the meaning of being human springs from the
truth that God has created and then assumed (in Christ) the very core
of human nature in all its weakness, sinfulness and growing pains as the
only, unique and full expression of God's own reality and self-communication. It follows then that all aspects of the world and of life contain
within them the tangible flesh of the Word of God.

> If the work of God was to flesh the Word, the Christian educator
> will forever be engaged in the task of Wording the flesh once
> again.

We all need to be convinced that the sacred and the secular are no longer
'over-against' each other, as though the divine were a superior counter-
attraction to the 'merely' human. This false notion springs from a
graceless dualism. For many centuries we have been using a kind of
language and a set of concepts in which the secular means 'that which
is not holy'. What is now needed is a shift in our images and vocabulary
so as to interpret the secular (in this case the independent autonomy and
total humanness of each student in swiftly changing times) in terms of
emergence and identity, and conceive of Christianity as the force and
grace which will remind, enable and compel the secular to be truly itself
– the holy work of God from the beginning. When creation and humanity are liberated by grace into their true identity, that identity is seen as
the immanent presence of God in all things, at all times and places.
Revealing and implementing this vision of the world as the precious
body of Christ is the work of catechists, teachers and preachers.

We need a shift in our images and vocabulary.

There are many obstacles to this precious work. For some strange and
even sinister reason, certainly one connected with the originally sinful
dimension of our being, so many are just not ready for this good news.
Disillusioned with their seemingly 'empty' lives, as they see it, people
are desperate for something else – an idealised version of their crea-
turehood, a superhuman type of existence, a fantasy of an impossible
wealth and an unreal beauty – beyond what they have and are. Toxic
shame, congenital envy, existential anxiety bring on a state of self-hate
and self-rejection that makes it impossible for millions to say 'yes' to
their basic humanity. The current, spiralling, and well-documented
incidence of serious depression and suicide among young and old is but
a soul-cry for a sense of love and meaning in their lives. An incarnational theology of humanity reveals how Jesus, the Human One, has
already said that difficult 'yes' to God for us. And he has also revealed
that deep within the light and darkness of each one's complicated

psyche, lie the graced seeds of the blossoming we dream about. People's lives are not empty; they are just not perceived, explored and lived under the mystery of incarnation.

There is nothing or nowhere, in fact, (except, perhaps, in a state of deliberately-chosen lovelessness) that these hidden graces do not exist. In Christian education, all subject matter is revealed as transformed in the light of revelation. Where formal school-work is concerned, for instance, the teaching of every subject across the curriculum would present unique opportunities for this revelation. In the perfectly integrated person of Jesus Christ all aspects of the Christian's life are made meaningful by love; they are explained and purified, they are intensified and multiplied.

> With incarnation, the true significance of existence entered the world. That significance was a person – the person of Christ, love personified.

All other dimensions of revelation are second-order sources and are taught only so as to point towards, and then experience, a glimpse of the truth of the mystery of incarnation.

Sacred scripture, for instance, can then be regarded as the original and normative testimony to the meaning of experience. In liturgy, the true meaning of creation and each one's personal destiny is affirmed and celebrated anew. In doctrines and dogmas we find the efforts of the Spirit-community to express the inexpressible and to formulate verbally for different people in different ages and from different cultures, some of the revealed wisdom of the Spirit concerning the purpose and significance of existence.

There will be great energy and excitement in the creating and crafting of approaches to religious educational work along these lines, where what we usually describe as the essential 'contents of the faith' (scripture, doctrine, liturgy, etc) will continue to be taught and remembered by the students. But first and foremost, the whole enterprise of catechesis in all its forms is to bring about, and to nurture, the promised 'abundance' of wisdom and joy in their lived lives. There are only a few vital questions to be remembered by teachers, catechists and priests – 'How will this approach bring a new, life-affecting inspiration and hope to others?' 'How can we catechise and teach our young people so that the quality of their lives is affected, and their attitudes and behaviour are altered?'

The whole enterprise of catechesis is to bring about, and to nurture, the promised 'abundance' of wisdom and joy in their lived lives.

Trinity and the Teenager

A recent Unicef survey revealed that Britain has the most troubled teenagers in Europe. If any section of our society is in need of immense compassion and support it is this vulnerable, gifted, potentially influential group. Yet there is mounting alarm in these islands at the unprecedented number of unprovoked attacks, of peer killings, of wanton destruction of property and the environment, perpetrated by young people.

Undoubtedly linked with those deeply disturbing facts is the widespread phenomenon of depression, stress, self-hatred and meaninglessness that is leading to what is currently called the 'cult and culture of suicide'. If social and cultural beliefs play a significant part in the frequency with which people are taking their own lives, can spiritual beliefs about how loved and precious they are begin to redeem them, to restore some of their lost dignity, sense of self-worth and hope?

How can our catechesis and religious education stimulate their curiosity about the mystery of the world around them, enthuse them with the sheer wonder of being alive, provide emotional security, a sense of identity, of belonging, of having a role, of being valued? Is there not bound to be a healing, saving grace at work amongst our troubled youngsters when the beautiful love-story of a compassionate God is gently revealed and shared with them by those catechists, teachers and preachers who themselves already believe that life-changing good news?

> We are all redeemed, in the end, by seeing our lives and our world through the lens of love.

Teachers often ask for examples of how the sacraments, for instance, or the teachings of the church can be presented in a way that has immediate and rich relevance for the lives of students. In our earlier consideration of the sacramental vision we briefly commented on the way the liturgy of the church, with reference to the Eucharist, heals and completes the brokenness of our daily lives. What follows here is a suggestion about how one of the main teachings of our faith might be explored so as bring about a transformation of attitude in our teenage students. *Fit for Mission? Schools* suggests that Catholic educators might be forgiven for seeing the mystery of the Most Holy Trinity as 'some exotic, theoretical subject that is totally irrelevant to the lives of staff and pupils.' (p 31)

Beyond a mere learning about it, and the effort to believe it, how does the doctrine of the Trinity, in the words of Pope Benedict, 'humanise and transform' the world of our young people, in all their hopes and mistakes, their dreams, failures and emptiness, as Pope John Paul II put it? How can this central mystery reveal some insights into the nature of God and of humanity so as to deepen the awareness of the love and meaning at the heart of the students' lives? When so many of their superstar heroes and heroines are helplessly hooked on drugs, often taking their own lives, how can they be helped to view themselves and the world around them through sacramental eyes? How can the Trinitarian formulation be shown to have a significance for, and a relevance to, their search for deeper meaning?

We begin, with our young adults, by looking at *God as Father*. There is a growing body of evidence pointing to the fact that father-teenage relationships in this country may be the most important influence of psychosocial health in older children. The acceptance of God as Father induces in the Christian a transformation of consciousness towards the world. It reveals that the author of reality is not hostile or indifferent. The ground of being is not a wasteland. The universe, in spite of much evidence to the contrary, is fundamentally a friendly place. The ultimate principle of total reality is love itself. There *is* meaning and purpose in life. Christians are now aware that they are sons and daughters, not isolated ciphers. They have a destiny. Their fear is transcended.

This is a huge breakthrough for many young people today. A Christian teenager may then say, 'In spite of my isolation and self-rejection; in spite of the meaningless of my life; in spite of temptation to exploit a hostile world for my own ends, belief in God as Father offers me, as daughter, the possibility of growing and sharing, of believing in myself and my unique destiny, of accepting, rejoicing in and loving myself.'

To believe that *God is Word* is to believe that we are listeners. One cannot come to self-knowledge alone. Each person must be told who they are by another. Our students are well aware of what is learned through relationships. Revelation happens. Because God's Word was fully enunciated in Christ the human creature, the Christian recognises that all creatures and experiences are revelatory. Sacramental listening happens when God's voice, God's Word is heard everywhere. Marvellously, Jesus Christ was both the uttered Word of God and the listening ear of humanity. Thoughtful teenagers do not reject or ridicule such explanations. We have known them to be influenced and moved by such revelations.

The Christian, then, remains open to the divine whisper of an incarnate God, speaking in all events and experiences. She hears in Christ the meaning offered to every human life with its pain and glory – that death and resurrection are the passage way to self-transcendence – death to our destructive drives, resurrection to the abundant life of grace in the here and now. A new hope is born, a passion for the possible. Already sensing their responsibility for protecting life, a careful respect for all created things grows gradually stronger in our young people through this realisation of our Christ-likeness; a rich sense of how central the issues of peace and justice are, the sacredness of all life, the closeness of God to a beloved world.

To understand *God as Spirit* is to know oneself as invited into the dance between Father and Son. This is a deeply moving truth, a holy sense of being caught up into the intimate rhythm of the Trinity. Our whole horizon of self-awareness, our experience of the dynamism of God's essence, is clarified and nourished. The free flowing of the Spirit refreshes and enlivens the dammed and stagnant waters of our jaded souls. Teenagers are no strangers to feelings of intense emptiness. Yet the mystic in them is waiting. Dead spirit comes to life; fear is transformed by love. They know themselves to be a part of something greater, a vital and precious finite image of the eternal God. This good news nourishes young hearts with their innate capacity for great vision, their readiness to participate in challenging causes.

The belief in God as Spirit creates life out of our death, draws us from our isolation and loneliness into the table of community, increases our energy through participation and belonging. The Spirit's essence is a dynamic relationship of love, beckoning and inspiring a passion and a freedom in those young human hearts – hearts that are broken and unsure because of volatile and fragmented family structures and manipulating media advertising. When desperate thoughts and tendencies towards suicide are threatening fragile psyches, a strong sense of God as comforting, constant Spirit can bring a life-restoring healing and trust to a confused and distressed soul. The mystery of the Trinity guarantees to those young and marginalised victims among us that God is truly family, and, whether they know it or not, that they are all born, baptised and always welcomed, no matter what, into that safe home.

Loaves and Hyacinths

The OTWTL document offers the notion of the Catholic sacramental imagination as a potential grounding for all the processes of transmission, particularly those of religious education, catechesis and formation. 'This would mean developing this sacramental imagination with the theology that underpins it as the core conceptual structure for all the cognitive elements of educational and formational programmes.'[25]

Many wise religious educationalists emphasise that without recourse to an artistic dimension in the stimulation of the sacramental imagination, our achievements will be very limited. The authors of OTWTL write of the 'poiesis' and aesthetic form of Christian living and of education. 'The practice of faith in all its forms is the participation in the beauty that God is, and it is also the constant creative disclosure of that beauty in the world. Thus art, in all its modes, is not something that is a luxury but the very living out of the vision of God. For this reason, the aesthetic of the life of faith is integral to the sacramental vision and it is also integral to religious education, catechesis and formation, but especially to evangelisation.'[26]

The task is not simple; nor is there only one way. Karl Barth held that, 'Theology is like attempting to paint a bird in flight – not that it is impossible or undesirable, but if we attempt to capture the complexity of the living God by what we know to be the limitations of human experience, we should not expect to arrive at any immutable rules or revelations.' We need to stay persevering, and very humble.

Sir Alec Clegg was Chief Education Officer for the West Riding of Yorkshire in the eighties. A widely-respected visionary, he was concerned about the neglect of 'the spirit' in educational trends across the curriculum. He saw spirituality in education as the nourishing of depth in relationship – with oneself, with others and with the world itself. Education includes the instilling of an awareness of love and meaning everywhere. It is the setting for the maturing of the students' humanity. He quoted a favourite verse of his aunt, a teacher:

If thou of fortune be bereft
And of thine earthly store hath left
Two loaves, sell one, and with the dole
Buy hyacinths to feed the soul.[27]

Clegg identified three categories of 'content' in education. In the first place, there are the two loaves, the facts that the student has to learn. A characteristic of this kind of learning is that the student gets it right or wrong; the accuracy can be measured. Then there is the category where the loaves and hyacinths are mixed. A student learns the 'Ode to Autumn' or he dances a Highland Fling. He can get the words of the Ode right or wrong, and this is a matter of loaves; but how expressively he recites or how elegantly he dances, the zest, the eagerness and artistry which he brings to the activities, is a matter of hyacinths. To some extent, at least, a new stirring has happened inside him.

But how do we increase the occasions when, maybe after a worthwhile and moving occasion, the student can bring to expression, in a person-ally intense way, the transformation that has taken place within his soul? He may give form to his personal epiphany in writing, poetry, paint, clay or movement. When this happens the hyacinths stand alone. While Clegg acknowledges the necessary balance between the cognitive and the affective, the left brain and the right, knowledge and wisdom, the technique and the dance, he would hold that the things of the spirit, the blossoming of the soul, the realisation of the spiritual self, are the true aims even of secular education. In our church schools we have the loaves; where do we water the hyacinths?

'I would suggest,' said Archbishop Vincent Nichols, 'that the starting point for much spiritual development is precisely in the development of all those aspects of living which "take us outside of ourselves" in the appreciation of beauty, goodness and truth ... The opportunity to be absorbed in an experience of beauty, or in a creative endeavour such as music or art, literature, science or drama, demonstrates at a deep exper-iential level the capacity of the human being to transcend herself or himself, to be drawn "outside" ...'[28] At the heart of all evangelising and catechising there is a non-rational element that cannot be conceptual-ised, and that therefore is in great danger of being lost in the pressurised world of education today.

In *The Religious Education Journal* of the seventies, John Westerhoff, Professor of Religion and Education at Duke University, wrote: 'Religion belongs to the sphere of the unsayable. It is better sung than recited, better danced than believed, better painted than talked about. That is why religious education is dependent on the arts. That is why children can have religious experience and, more importantly, can help adults who have become independent, rational and productive, to redis-cover the holy.'

Even in pre-Vatican Council days, Bernard Lonergan and Jaques Maritain emphasised, in their references to the process of education, the necessary role of a free exploration of art and of the emotions. This exploration, they say, is what keeps our lives and the world in tune with God. Lonergan claims that 'the life we are living is a product of artistic creation' and that it is on the artistic, symbolic level that we live our full range of humanity, discovering that we can become 'emergent, ecstatic, standing out ... originating freedom'.[29]

This exploration is what keeps our lives and the world in tune with God.

Theologian of beauty, Hans Urs Von Balthasar sees music as the most ineffable art because it is the most immediate. That is why he sees its role on the cusp between humanity and divinity. 'Music is a borderland of the human,' he wrote, 'and it is here that the divine begins.' He sees music, particularly Mozart's, as liminal, between that which can and cannot be spoken, between God and humanity, between Creator and creation.[30]

But even in this pressurised world of competitive education, we can still learn from our 'secular' colleagues. In so far as our own schools are concerned, among the preparatory literature for an OFSTED inspection is a plea for encouraging the uses of imagination in teaching and learning. One of the aims espoused is the developing and transformation of intuition and insight so that students are moved by beauty and stay open to what 'lies beyond'.

How can students be inspired to express their inmost, spiritual potential while schools are driven by merit-lists, points and league-tables? 'Were they (students) not able to be moved by wonder at the beauty of the world we live in, or the power of artists, musicians and stories of writers, they would live in an inner spiritual and cultural desert.' (National Curriculum Council Paper, 1993). Aware of how current pressures can reduce teaching and learning to a merely cerebral exercise, many DES papers encourage a more creative and imaginative use of life-themes and cross-subject weaving in an effort to restore a more whole-school energy and motivation. (e.g. *Excellence and Enjoyment*, 2005)

Summary

'I have come very strongly to believe that it is the cultivation of imagination which should be the chief aim of education. We have a duty to educate the imagination above all else.' (Mary Warnock)

OTWTL recommends the developing of the 'sacramental imagination with the theology that underpins it as the core conceptual structure for all the cognitive elements of educational and formational programmes.'

The Hebrew and Christian scriptures are our canon of the imagination, the standard and guide for Christian imagining. They are stories sprung from stirred imaginations, as God's people remembered and envisioned their relationship with the Lord invisible among them.

In the perennial task of handing on the faith, nothing is more needed than that parents and pastors, catechists and communi-

ties rekindle in themselves the flame of the Christian imagination. (– from the thought of John Henry Newman)

The catechist works within the intrinsic relationship between the
students' life experience and the specifically revelatory dimension of Christianity.

Humanity can never be the measure of itself; 'Christ is the completion of the human project.' (OTWTL)

Teachers and catechists need to be at home with a theology of
creation that provides a basis for a Christ-centred humanism.

If the work of God in the beginning was to flesh the Word, the
work of the catechist now is to Word the flesh once again. Words
alone cannot carry such a vision. Artistic expression is needed for
its implementation in human hearts.

Religious education is dependent upon the arts. 'Music and
singing are the borderland of the human. It is here that the divine
begins.' (Hans Urs Von Balthasar)

The religious educator must be an artist who is deeply in touch
with the genius of the Catholic imagination. Her primary function is to hold up to the people of God the great images, stories
and pictures of salvation that are at the heart of the Christian
tradition.

The ministry of catechesis serves to name, in ritual, symbol and
word, the grace that we experience in daily life, at the same time
purifying and deepening that graced experience.

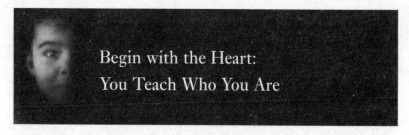

Begin with the Heart:
You Teach Who You Are

'Know yourself because you teach who you are.' Teaching, catechising and preaching, like most truly human activities, are fundamentally coloured and textured by the state of our inner lives. Where involvement with the spreading of the Word is concerned, this truth assumes a huge importance. Invisibly and silently, we are always projecting the condition of our souls through everything we say and do. 'Viewed from this angle,' observes Parker J. Palmer, 'teaching holds a mirror to the soul.' This section emphasises that the more confident, sure-footed and aware we are around our own emotions and attitudes, the more effective we will be in our catechising and in our own living out of the faith. It is only then that the evangeliser, like a mid-wife, will be in a position to draw forth from students their own precious essence – the image of God.

The key to effective RE or catechesis does not lie in the crafting of the perfect curriculum or syllabus. We do not necessarily have to re-write immediately, in the light of a theology of nature and grace, an updated syllabus to procure the results we sincerely hope for. *It will not come from a book. It can only come from a person. It is the catechist's own heart that must first be re-created; the teacher's own vision that must first be transformed.* If it is true that 'the teacher does not write on inanimate material, but on the very spirits of human beings',[31] then the first writing must be written across the teacher's own heart. Once God's signature is identified and cherished there, everything that springs from that place will be blessed. 'Where to begin?' the twelfth century mystic Meister Eckhart was asked. 'Begin with heart.'

A popular catch-phrase of the past held that 'faith is caught, rather than taught'. This is still substantially true. It does not always mean that the faith has to be taught *as well as* to be caught. In the graced teaching is the catching and in the catching is the teaching. In the blessed knowing is the loving and in the loving is the knowing. It is a dialogue of life.

However, if the imaginative vision of which we speak is to be 'caught' as well as 'taught', how much expectation is riding on the personal charism and passion of the catechist or teacher? We usually 'catch' things from people with charisma. So very many people today will testify to their memories of a former teacher, who while being unutterably herself, was also alive with a love for her subject. As St Augustine advocated, she loved both what she taught and whom she taught. '... what we have loved others will love, and we will teach them how.'[32]

Can those seeds which hopefully blossom during the later life of the student, only take root in the first place, when, in one of those many potentially Emmaus moments, 'heart speaks to heart'? When the poet Mark Van Doren was asked to name his finest teacher, he surprised himself by selecting one who didn't teach him anything that he ever remembered. He wondered why:

> The style, the style's the trick that keeps him kept –
> no, not a trick; it must unfold as grace, inevitably, necessarily,
> as tomcats stretch: in such a way he lolled upon his desk
> and fell in love again before our very eyes
> again, again – how many times again! –
> with Dante, Chaucer, Shakespeare, Milton's Satan,
> as if his shameless, glad, compelling love
> were all he really wanted us to learn;
> no, that's not right; we were occasionals
> who lucked or stumbled or were pushed on him –
> he fell in love because he fell in love;
> we were but windfall parties to those falls.[33]

Anthony de Mello tells a helpful story. An explorer returned from the Amazon was pressed by his people to describe to them his adventure. But he struggled to find words that could depict the flowers of breath-taking beauty that he alone had seen, or the danger he sensed in his heart as he heard wild beasts or sinister paddles in treacherous stretches of the rivers. He told them to go and explore for themselves. To help them he drew a map. But instead of undertaking the journey themselves, the only way to experience first hand the wonders of what the explorer had experienced, most students settled for the map. Those with personal copies considered themselves Amazon experts because they knew by heart every twist and turn of the rivers. They formed a little club to study more, to look at photographs, and even dress like the inhabitants of that area. And that was as far as they got. Only later did some of them realise that they had missed the whole point of the enterprise.[34]

The map is necessary, but secondary. It is a means, not an end. It must be transcended, not exaggerated. It is only when the students' hearts are transformed and filled with excitement, that the explorer's work is done. It is only when the listeners themselves are somehow transported into that enchanted land of the adventurer's stories, that the true mission will have been accomplished. What was missing from the approach of the students was the use of their imagination. There was no excitement of vision, no enchantment of their desire. 'God guard me from the thoughts men think,' wrote W. B. Yeats, 'in the mind alone; he that sings a lasting song, thinks in a marrow bone.'

In *Theology in its new Context*, Bernard Lonergan wrote about the radical transformation that happens when the student actually experiences the truth of theology. As well as a deep change in her apprehension and values, a greater change happens in herself, in her relationships to other persons, and in her relationship to God. 'The person apprehends differently, values differently, relates differently, because they have become different ... The old order has gone, and a new order has begun (2 Cor 5:17).'

Michael Paul Gallagher reminds us of Joseph Campbell's conviction that we cannot teach people into believing. All we can do is share with them the radiance of our own discoveries. He also quotes Sebastian Moore who said that theology has to be autobiographical if it is to enflame the heart with love of God.[35] It is out of the fullness of our own hearts that our words will touch others. It is only to the extent that the reader at Mass, 'like a fifth gospel', is sharing the words of scripture as though they were love-letters, that the listeners will be deeply affected.

> It is only to the extent that the catechist has small but true glimpses of the mystery of her own inner world that she will open the hearts of her students to the mystery of their worlds too.

Know Yourself Well because you Teach Who you Are

Because we are all wonderfully designed by God, so carefully and lovingly put together, we have astonishing capacities to influence and transform each other at profound levels of our living. It is like a vibrant network of mutual interconnectedness, a flow of energy and inner power that began in creation and was revealed and personified in Jesus at the incarnation. A theology of nature and grace concerns itself with such graced experiences in the unfolding of our humanity and of creation itself, an unfolding that is the continuing fleshing out in time and space of the implications of the once-for-all moment when God became human. When it comes to effective catechesis, formation and teaching, so much depends on the purified humanity of the educators. No music can be created from an out-of-tune violin. No beauty greets the eye through the cracked and blurred panes of a broken window. *Nemo dat quod non habet.*

No one can give what they have not got.

'In order to play the prophetic role which education for liberation desperately needs, educators first need to become mystics themselves, to recover their own potential for contemplation, wonder, stillness, relationship with the natural world, and a thirst for learning which transcends narrow curriculum limits.'[36] Otherwise the process of catechising will be conducted from the outside in. It will be an objective exercise with no engagement of the heart. The fire will be missing. There is something intensely personal about the interchange that happens in sharing the good news. It is as though Jesus was revealing something of his own self every time he explained things to those around him. Heart spoke to heart whenever they gathered to search for the Father's love and meaning hidden in the gift of their lives.

In other words, the catechist can only be really present to someone else to the same extent as she is present to herself. She can only understand another to the same extent as she understands herself. She can only walk the Emmaus journey with others to the extent that she has walked it within her own heart. It is only when she has travelled the twists and turns of the labyrinth of her own holy mystery that she can be a grace for another in her teaching and in her presence.

Until teachers have faced the demons and shadows in their own psyche there will always be something superficial and even misleading in the way they encounter others, personally in love or professionally in service. It is only to the extent that any of us know ourselves, that we can begin to glimpse anything of God. It is well to remember the *noverim me, noverim te* of St Augustine. 'I seek to know myself, O Lord, so that I may know thee all the more.'

Good teaching cannot ever be reduced to the latest curriculum or set of sacramental guidelines, or pedagogical technique. It comes from the self-knowledge, the authenticity and integrity of the catechist, the preacher, the teacher. Every major document on the effectiveness of Christian education in all its forms insists on that non-negotiable premise. This is not about the need to be perfect; it is about the need to be aware – aware of our inner dividedness, of our fears and shadows, of the unfamiliar terrain of our own complex interiority. The hidden self is notoriously shy of the light.

There is a world within you no one has ever seen,
A voice no one has ever heard – not even you.
And yet, unknown, you are your own seer, your own interpreter.
And so, with eyes and ears grown sharp for voice or sign,
Listen well. Not to these words but to that inward voice,
That impulse beating in your heart like a far wave.
Turn to that source and you will find what no one has ever found,
A ground within you that no one has ever seen,
A world beyond the limits of your dream horizon.[37]

Know yourself because you teach and catechise who you are. Jesus revealed that true ministry is found only in the individual and community that can accept their own vulnerability. We all find that a hard thing to do; and so does the institutional church itself. 'The church is an evangeliser but she begins by being evangelised herself. She has a constant need of being evangelised if she wishes to retain freshness, vigour and strength in order to proclaim the gospel.'[38] We have no choice about this principle. It is the way of incarnation.

What the world and the church need today, to quote Pope John Paul II once more, 'are heralds of the gospel who are experts in humanity, who know the depths of their human hearts, who can share the joys, hopes, agonies and distress of people today, and who are, at the same time, contemplatives who have fallen in love with God.'

Without such 'expertise', especially around the fundamental woundedness at the heart of our lives, there will be something vital missing in our attempts to spread the good news of salvation. That vulnerability, in fact, is the essential aspect of our humanity that God needed in Jesus, and now needs in us, to make the divine gift of power in our powerlessness tangible and visible to a suffering world. There is no other way. It is only through failure that the path opens up. 'There is something deeply theological here,' *On the Threshold* reminds us, 'Brokenness is actually central to our faith. We believe in a Lord who came to triumph through brokenness. Can we expect anything else? ... We are inviting people to experience the all-powerful, risen and triumphant Lord but who is discovered in the weakness, the brokenness and the pain of our inner and outer world. It opens new avenues for all of us to realise afresh that we are initiated into the life of the wounded healer.'[39]

In one of his first homilies, Pope Benedict very bravely admitted his own frailty and sinfulness in the face of the daunting challenge he had accepted. He emphasised the necessity for such self-knowledge so as to be perceived all the more clearly as a sacrament of God's mercy and goodness. 'The catechist must come to Christ with his unrest and uncertainty and even his weakness and sinfulness, his life, his death. He must, so to speak, enter into Christ with all his own self, he must "appropriate" Christ and assimilate the whole of the reality of the incarnation and redemption.'[40]

> The catechist must come to Christ with his unrest and uncertainty and even his weakness and sinfulness, his life, his death.

Forging in the Smithy of the Soul

To embrace vulnerability is to surrender to a kind of dying. It is easier to leave our life unexamined. Too many shadows and weaknesses surface when we stop to take stock of our deepest emotions. Once we begin to unblock the flow of our suppressed memories and feelings, the flood-gates open. We fear we may be swept away. It is not always easy to hold our life together. We are full of contradictions. It takes a brave heart to ask the dangerous questions: 'Is there really a lot of joy in my life?', 'Do I really believe the love that I profess?', 'Am I an authentic person, always trying to tell the truth?', 'Am I living and teaching out of my ego or my essence, out of the "what" of my life rather than the "who" of it?'

Something in us desperately resists this admission of woundedness and brokenness. The ego is offended at this kind of dying. It fights hard to hold its control. So do many ecclesiastical systems. But the work of the catechist is about humble service, not about brokering power. Beyond the well-crafted words and practised skills, the catechist's effectiveness arises from her very being, from the gratitude always welling up inside her, from a love that is nourished by a forgiveness so graciously granted, from a palpable joy that never goes away for long.

We must *become* the salvation that Jesus has won for us; we must carry in our bodies and souls the new life that God extravagantly fills us with. Without the personal experience of faith, of having been redeemed, of dependence only on God's faithfulness, the catechist and teacher will struggle too hard to win over the minds of others. The words of life will become lifeless words. The servant will become the tyrant. Unless the catechist's own heart is nourished, how can she nurture the hearts of others? Without regular reflection on these priorities, without daily meditation to protect what is precious within us, we would all begin to dominate rather than to serve.

> Unless the catechist's own heart is nourished, how can she nurture the hearts of others?

In this regard the final pages of *On the Threshold* provide much food for thought. 'Instead of a formal gateway, the sheep-fold had a hole in its perimeter wall through which the shepherd would guide his sheep in the evening, and across which he himself would lie down through the hours of darkness. The protecting gate was his own body, over which those within and without, might easily trample. He stayed outside the security of the sheepfold and remained, vulnerable, on its threshold.

This image carries no overtones of power, but eloquently expresses some of the feelings of helplessness and insecurity experienced by many who work in parish catechesis and school RE. To be on the threshold with people is to share with them their hopes and anxieties, to listen carefully and generously as they unfold the story of their own insecurities, to struggle with them to discern the next step. As we patiently remain with them, we become aware of the complexities of our own situation. We find ourselves awakened to our own uncertainties.

Far from finding that the threshold is a place of easy solutions, ready answers and distinct conclusions, all parties can emerge from it with further questions and a sense of unease and incompleteness. The threshold is, above all, a place of service – both to those who approach for guidance, and to the Lord in whose name we persevere in our commitment to God's work. Like Christ, we stand on the threshold: are we all-powerful doorkeepers who control, or humble threshold-companions who serve?'[41]

The heart of education is the heart of the educator.

Thomas Groome is the senior professor of theology and religious education at Boston College, USA. In *Forging in the Smithy of the Teacher's Soul* he explores the notion that 'the heart of education is the heart of the educator'.[42] The transforming energy of teaching and learning is subtle and spiritual. Groome writes of St Augustine's understanding of 'the teacher within' each person, proposing that when we learn something, the 'real' teacher is not the teacher on the outside but the one inside.

Augustine explained that the 'teacher within' is the divine presence at the core of the person, our own souls. Groome refers to Parker J. Palmer, an internationally respected educational expert, who has taken the Augustinian proposal one step further by explaining that 'the teacher within the teacher awakens the teacher within the student'. Maybe this is another way of emphasising the biblical belief in the notion of 'heart speaking to heart'?

Carol Barry, who lectures in theology and religious education at St Patrick's College of Dublin University, admits to being a great admirer of Dr Palmer as well. She quotes him: 'Spirituality – the human quest for connectedness – is not something that needs to be brought into or "added to" the curriculum. It is at the heart of every subject we teach, where it waits to be brought forth.' And again, 'How can we take heart in teaching once more so that we can, as good teachers always do, give our heart to our students? How can we who teach, reclaim our hearts, for the sake of our students, ourselves, and educational reform?'[43]

In his celebrated *The Courage to Teach*, Palmer writes, 'Teaching, like any truly human activity, emerges from our inwardness, for better or worse. As I teach, I project the condition of my soul on to my students, my subjects and our way of being together.' In other words, the way we teach, preach, evangelise reflects the state of our own hearts and souls. Enabling and inspiring catechists and teachers is not always about pro-viding maps, charts and syllabuses. It mostly consists in helping them understand that the essential teaching and catechising flows from the quality and integrity of their own inner life. 'Teaching holds a mirror to the soul. Knowing myself is as crucial to good teaching as knowing my students and my subject. When I do not know myself, I cannot know who my students are.'[44] But knowing and being who you are require relentless effort across the span of life.

The way we teach, preach, evangelise reflects the state of our own hearts and souls.

It takes intense discipline to stay vigilant so as to spot the tricks of the ego. Dying to one's vanity is a death indeed. Without regular contem-plation it is difficult to discern the sources of our 'good deeds'. Clarifying our vision is hard spiritual work. It is worth reminding our-selves again of the questions put by Archbishop Rowan Williams when speaking to all lay ministers of the gospel: 'Are you attending to your vision? Are you stripping yourself in prayer before the terrible and searching Word of God? Are you being refined in that fire? And am I? Is my vision doing that to me, breaking and remaking my thoughts and words, breaking my heart and my mind? We Christians have the right, perhaps the duty, to put these questions to each other and to hear them from each other.'

Where there's no vision within there will be little light for the world without. In *Writers, Critics, and Children* Ted Hughes wrote; 'The inner world, separated from the outer world, is a place of demons. The outer world, separated from the inner world, is a place of meaningless objects and machines. The faculty that makes the human being out of these two worlds is called divine. That is only a way of saying that it is the faculty without which humanity cannot really exist. It can be called religious or visionary. More essentially, it is imagination which embraces both outer and inner worlds in a creative spirit.'

Midwives of Mystery

There are many striking titles with which to honour catechists and teachers. They all reveal a range of roles that come into play when the adventure of education is undertaken. Once the work of the educator is understood at the deeper levels of divine and human mystery, a new reverence for the vocation of teaching follows. The late Cardinal Hume referred to teaching as the highest calling. It is the privileged, difficult work of discovering and revealing the image of God in students of all ages. That is why teachers and catechists may be celebrated as midwives of mystery; they bring God's beauty to birth in those they serve. The poet A. S. J. Tessimond writes:

> Man can be taught perhaps only
> That which he already knows
> For only in the soul that is ready
> Grows the mind's obstinate rose;
> The right word at the wrong time
> Is wind-caught, blown away;
> And the most the ages' sages'
> Wisdom and wit can say,
> Is no more to the quickest pupil
> Than a mid-wife's delicate steady
> Fingers aiding and easing
> The thought half-born already.[45]

Once a catechist sees her work along these lines of meaning, once her understanding of her ministry is perceived in these images of bringing something precious to birth, then everything about her presence to her students will be transformed. But first the veils must be parted for her own vision to be clear and focused. Without that first transformation in her own heart, there will be no wonder for her students to catch. 'First *become* the change you want to see in the world' said Gandhi; the rest follows.

In a somewhat similar way, the teacher and catechist can be called *prisms of love* as they reveal the colours of God in everybody and everything in the life of the student. When the catechist is alive to rumours of God's accessibility everywhere, and sensitive to the divine presence in every presence, he will lose no opportunity to penetrate carefully the disguises of God in all the happenings of each one's life – even in the murky and sinful places. As a prism reveals the colours of the spectrum in ordinary white light, the enlightened teacher will draw out from the hearts of the students, the rainbows of originality waiting to be released. For such a catechist even the most 'ordinary' moments will become near-occasions of grace – 'turn but a stone and start a wing'.

In this sense the teacher can also be called a *minder of thresholds*. Even where experiences may be seen as negative or even destructive, they can still be identified as places of grace. These can be hugely significant moments of breakthrough in the lives of young and old. God can only deal with reality. Thomas Merton said that every moment is a gateway to heaven, a threshold to God's heart. This holds true for all the subjects taught and all the experiences that happen in the context of school and parish.

Co-creators with God is a beautiful title for all those workers in the vineyard. The catechist and teacher, by inspiring creativity and imagination in each student, empower them to be the prophetic voice of a Christian counter-culture, to be reflective and critical in a world that so easily loses its way and its wonder. *Agents of transformation* is another appropriate name for those committed to establish the reign of God. What is hoped and prayed for is a transformed attitude to life on the part of the students, a longing for true ecumenical and inter-faith trust and harmony in a suspicious religious milieu, a new vision about the holiness of the earth, a passion for identifying the conformity and consumerism all around us, and a yearning for peace in a world of wars.

True education has been described as 'resistance to closure'. When dealing with mystery this is the only appropriate catechetical approach. *Angels of openness* is a title that could well be applied to teachers and catechists. They protect the limitlessness of God by refusing all definitions as final. Thomas Aquinas saw the quality of 'magnanimity', a first cousin to openness, as God's main attribute; and, by the same token, designated the deliberately parsimonious or stingy ('pusillanimity') as bordering on sinfulness.

It takes great courage to remain open under the controlling pressure to be certain.

In a national address to Catholic teachers some years ago, Bishop David Konstant reminded them of 'the great need to integrate wholly what we believe with how we live. In Christian teachers there is need for real personal integration and harmony, so that the truth we teach is a genuine reflection of the person that we are.'[46] He went on to quote Pope Paul VI: 'Modern man listens more willingly to witnesses than to teachers, and if he does listen to teachers, it is because they are also witnesses.'[47]

The Spirituality of Teaching and Catechising

'Teaching has an extraordinary spiritual depth and is one of humanity's excellent and creative activities, for the teacher (or catechist) does not write on inanimate material, but on the very spirits of human beings.'[48] The Catholic tradition has always preserved a profound respect for, and a unique understanding of, the sacredness of teaching and learning. Even more so does it honour the holiness of those who educate, and of those who listen and hear. This sensitivity to the holiness of humanity establishes 'the ground on which to stand' – a ground that takes its terms of reference from the incarnation.

No other religious body or denomination has honoured the central place of the humanity of Christ as the Catholic tradition has. This is the enduring revelation of Christianity. The authors of OTWTL emphasise the need to remember the church's dedication to the human, to reclaim 'a Christian humanism'. In the *Religious Dimensions of Education in a Catholic School* (CES) we read, 'Catholic schools (and all catechesis) work to foster the Christian understanding of the human person as made in the image and likeness of God. We nurture the human wholeness of each student to play a full role in society – fully human and fully alive for self and others, providing a community in which faith, culture and life are brought into harmony'. This is a unique vision and an overpowering revelation; it is why we speak about 'the spirituality' of teaching and catechising.

Christian education in all its modes and models is always meant to be about the growth, development and journey of the whole human person towards abundant life, as a unique creation made in God's image. 'At the heart of Catholic education and catechesis lies the Christian vision of the human person, of the entire potential of every student, made, as each one is, in the image and likeness of God.'[49] Therefore, whenever a catechist, teacher or priest is opening the mind and heart of a child or adult to the wonder of themselves and of nature, no matter what the topic, content or context, or whenever a parent, governor or domestic staff member is carefully and lovingly attentive to each one's needs, they are, in fact, and often unknowingly, uncovering for another the holiness of every moment; they are completing the work of Jesus in incarnating God more fully into this world.

> To facilitate young people's growing in wisdom and age is to watch the unfolding of God in our midst.

To see a child smiling as it pronounces or spells a new word is to see something of the joy of the incarnate God. The educationalist Jerome

Bruner once suggested that it is not so much children's birthdays we should be celebrating as their moments of breakthrough into fresh connecting and understanding. The transcendence by the child of each of its formative stages of development is a sacrament of divine energy that is worthy of special notice and celebration.

Rachael Kessler, Director of the Institute for Social and Emotional Learning in the United States, carried out some research into the spiritual drives and needs of teenage students. Kessler devotes her book *The Soul of Education: Helping Students Find Connection, Compassion and Character at School* to a study of her findings.[50] After many years of questions and stories, a pattern began to emerge. She offers seven gateways to the soul of students, even of the 'less promising' ones:

• The search for meaning and purpose
• The longing for silence and solitude
• The urge for transcendence
• The hunger for joy and delight
• The creative drive
• The call for initiation
• The yearning for deep connection[51]

When the catechist believes that the ministry of teaching is about revealing the divine humanity within each student, then, already, the whole enterprise is seen to be sacred. To enter this sacred work wholeheartedly the teacher must be forever open to the self-transformation that gives inspiration and confidence to the emerging vision of the students. Ultimately the source of this vision, inspiration and transformation is the humanity of Jesus. And just as Jesus had to purify his own humanity to save the world (Jn: 17:19), so will the teacher.

The Heart of a Teacher/Catechist/Leader

What can be said about the self-aware, self-transcending catechist, teacher, leader in parish or school? She is someone who is capable of holding within herself the tension of the paradoxes of life. She knows that the greater the soul, the greater the shadow. She does not always require certainty but can live with unknowing and mystery. She does not need to be always 'right', in charge of, or in roles of command and decision-making. She is ready to empty the cupboards of her life of titles, offices and public importance. She knows who she is when everything is taken away. She has learned the hard truth that only her authentic self will eventually and always win through. She sees herself as a co-creator with God in her demanding work of education.

The catechist is liberated enough to be care-full and be care-free, because he knows he is not alone. He is free because he knows that God is greater than any system or organisational structure. He is free because, while he strives with every fibre of his being to make his school or parish community a place of collaborative ministry and compassion, he can do so without undue stress, fear or anxiety. Aware of his own fallibility and weaknesses, he does not judge or condemn either colleague or competitor. He learns to pray quickly for patience rather than to say words that take ages to retract. He is well aware that what he does not transform within himself, he will transmit outwards. What is not inwardly healed is projected on to others.

The teacher is trying to live by a simple but difficult wisdom, where to be authentic, transparent and open is more important than to be successful, obeyed or respected. She can now tell the difference between acting out of her ego and acting out of her essence. Because of her daily habits of reflection and prayer, she is finding new spaces in her soul to deepen her inner life and her outward personality. She is finding a vibrant zest for life in the middle of her increasing work-load. She does not lose heart for long because she sees her work within a bigger picture. This means that, whatever the immediate outcomes of her life's efforts, against the infinite horizon of God's acres, nothing is wasted and everything is harvested.

Summary

'Know yourself well because you teach who you are.' Our effectiveness as teachers and catechists is inextricably linked with our self-awareness and self-knowledge.

The catechist can only be really present to someone else to the same extent that she is present to herself.

Good teaching cannot ever be reduced to the latest curriculum, or set of creeds, or pedagogical technique – it depends, for the greater part, on the purified, enthusiastic humanity of the educator. 'There is no greater calling on earth than teaching.' (Cardinal Hume)

'Modern man listens more willingly to witnesses than to teachers; and if he does listen to teachers, it is because they are also witnesses.' (Pope Paul VI)

'The teacher or catechist does not write on inanimate material but on the very spirit of human beings.' (CES)

There is a spirituality of teaching and of learning, of the catechist and of the student. This spirituality remains constant only when Christ is kept at the centre.

'Within Christian spirituality, long before we speak of anything else – church, dogmas, commandments, even admonitions to love and justice – we must speak about Jesus, the vine, the blood, the pulse, the person and energy that undergirds everything else.' (Ronald Rolheiser)

Beyond set programmes, courses and syllabuses, it takes whole-hearted participation in the whole church to form students in the faith. Without belonging to an enthusiastic community beyond school and family, it will be so difficult for a student to experience a living faith and a vibrant church.

Courageous Conversations

How would you describe the tangible transformation that a theology of nature and grace, and of the sacramental imagination, brings to teaching and catechising?

In a revised curriculum, how would topics such as church, sacraments, prayer, particular themes and issues be presented in such a way as to be true to the theology, the sacramental vision, the Christian humanism as presented in OTWTL?

How did you respond to the discussion about the way church teachings and human experience need each other in the presentation of the faith?

How can a living, intelligible and necessary theology of nature and grace be made accessible to teachers and catechists across the dioceses?

Is it reasonable to expect catechists and teachers to be people with passion and conviction, to be on fire with their responsibility, to transform the students by the power of their energy, vision and compassion? Is it true to say that you teach, catechise, lead (serve) and preach 'who you are'?

How can the *raison d'être* of the RE Dept in a Post-Primary School be redefined and augmented, e.g. in contributing to, and in facilitating the sacramental vision in the teaching of all subjects and in all that happens within the school community?

How do you respond to these quotations from P.J. Parker's *The Courage to Teach?*:

- 'If we want to grow as teachers, we must learn to talk to each other about our inner lives, our own identity and integrity.'
- 'Good teaching cannot be reduced to technique; good teaching comes from the identity and integrity of the teacher.'
- 'Good teachers possess a capacity for connectedness – woven between themselves, their subjects and their students, on the loom of the heart.'
- 'My ability to connect with my students, and to connect them with the subject, depends less on the methods I use than on the degree to which I know and trust my selfhood – and am willing to make it available and vulnerable in the service of learning.'

- 'The best gift we receive from the great mentors is not their knowledge or their approach to teaching but the sense of self they evoke within us.'
- 'Teaching and learning are ultimately grounded in a sense of the sacred.'

A conversation about Catholic secondary schools

If it takes a village to raise a child, it takes the whole parish to raise a Catholic. '... the main task of handing on the faith is the whole community's task ...' (T. W. Tilley) Thomas Groome adds: 'If (passing on the faith) amounted to no more than teaching students what Christians believe – the cognitive content – then catechetical education could be done by some sort of schooling alone. But because being Christian pertains to a person's whole identity, and requires active membership in a community of disciples, a schooling model can help out but will not be sufficient. Though good instruction "in the faith" is imperative, it takes something more to form the Christian being of people.'

Groome continues: 'When we think of "handing on the faith" we simply must stop equating this with a school/programme project and instead reclaim the notion that all Christians are responsible for sharing their faith, and that catechetical education must be a communal effort that intentionally engages every Christian community – family, parish and bonded group ... there is no one programme for doing catechetical education; there is no sure or easy procedure for "handing on the faith".'[52]

If this is true, how realistic is it to expect an educational institution, which is now regarded as a vital focus and forum for nurturing the Catholic faith, but in which many of the staff belong to other denominations, and where many of the Catholics are not practising, to bring about a real transformation in the lives of the post-primary students who themselves are mostly not practising, and come from many different parish communities where they are generally not known, and with whom they have no sense of belonging? This bleak scenario of increasing separation brings anxiety and despondency.

And this is where the grace of courage and hope comes to our aid. Educators in the faith need to keep that very faith in mind when faced with a culture of non-belonging within the church and the world. Does a theology of nature and grace and the sacramental vision of the church provide food for reflection and conversation around this current, challenging situation?

Part Four

Engaging the World

Postmodernism is uneasy with all certainties, especially scientific and religious ones. There is no place for 'grand narratives' in a worldview that is associated with the unpredictable and the provisional. At the same time, many cultures and religions are fundamentally attached to their beliefs and practices, with little or no interest in ecumenical involvement. In both mind-sets there is often suspicion and even hostility. In the face of much intransigence and a pervading sense of chaos or even threat, is there any way forward for the Christian faith today? A theology of nature and grace will relish the opportunity of validating its claims in a postmodern, multicultural world. It would not be the first time that the incarnate God found new self-expression in a place of confusion, contradiction and aggression.

Nothing human is hurt by the gospel. Every authentic value, in whatever culture it appears, is accepted and raised by Christ.

Pope John Paul II

We still refer too easily to believers and non-believers as if believers had faith and non-believers had no faith. Faith is by no means an exclusively religious category. Faith, in fact, is an element that belongs intrinsically and universally to the human condition.

Dermot Lane

If we can acknowledge the human need for transcendence, and honour the ways in which created goodness expresses that need, then we are well placed to draw individual postmodern spiritualities into the larger 'story' of salvation history.

John Drane

It takes imagination, creativity and courage to renew our language of the kingdom as a home of all humanity – of all whose theological sympathies are different from our own - even when they appear to be going in the wrong direction. They have their own truth too. We must give authority to others. As Bishop Butler said, 'Let us not fear that truth can endanger truth.'

Timothy Radcliffe

Speaking appropriately of God is, while not impossible, the most difficult, the most demanding, the most dangerous thing that human speech can do ... It is the tragedy of modern Western culture to have fallen victim to the illusion that it is perfectly easy to talk about God.

Nicholas Lash

Then I remember that it is this world, this fragmented postmodern world, that God so loves, making possible again the search to uncover the seeds of the Word in contemporary circumstances, even if the latter bears many traces of elements that are inimical to the Christian gospel and way of life.

James Corkery

What can the church do for, or with, a young, post-Modern, post-Enlightenment, European generation? To batter them with church authority is more likely to alienate them than to persuade them. Better indeed, as Newman suggested, to ask them what they think.

Clifford Longley

One of the priceless treasures that we possess as Christians is that we know our story.

Bishop Edwin Regan

Postmodern and Multicultural: Befriending the Enemy

This section offers some common ground for courageous conversation. Such debate will point to the need for Christians to examine again their own beliefs and doctrines, and to reinterpret and purify the language and images around the mystery and reality we call God. For all postmodernism's and pluralism's undoubted potential for the erosion of the Christian faith from the world today, can there also be a hidden potential for the transformation of our understanding of the Christian faith, for the enrichment of our spirituality? 'Some theologians view postmodernity as not merely the friend of Christian faith, but "a cultural wavelength" in which faith can live and be credible today. To challenge prevalent social injustice Christian faith needs to re-appraise its own foundation symbols, and, in particular, its theology of creation.' (*Denis Carroll*)

For teachers, catechists and priests who were formed and trained in an earlier decade, the postmodern scenario right now can be very confusing. Many of us were part of a clear and structured organisation where, to put it mildly, the boundaries were non-negotiable. As one wag put it, 'Everything was either forbidden or compulsory!' The old enemies were well in our sights – the world, the flesh and the devil. In striking language Pope Pius IX's *Syllabus of Errors* had hammered out an unambiguous opposition to 'progress, liberalism and modern civilisation'. This was before 'situation ethics', having a 'subjective conscience', and 'making my own rules', became common in an *à la carte* type of church. It was before an unprecedented transformation in the world of communication and travel took place. It was also before a new confidence in personal opinion and a disregard for objective truth became widespread. It was becoming clear that, in the words of W .B. Yeats, 'the centre does not hold' any more.

Those old certainties and methods are disappearing. Many of us are now anxious about the very basics of our attempts to establish God's kingdom in our communities. Referring to the current situation in theatrical terms, a commentator said, 'The audience is restless and leaving the auditorium; the cast is not sure of the lines, even of the plot; and the microphones are not working!'

The OTWTL document convinces its readers that the evangelising and catechising ministers of the word, paid or voluntary, are currently facing major challenges on several fronts regarding the uses and limitations of language, the nature of knowledge and the preparation of more appropriate methodologies. These challenges arise a) from the phenomenon of diverse cultures, religions, and their values, as embodied in the young and older students whom we serve in our parishes today; b) from the alarming complexities of what is called a postmodern society; and c) from the real difficulties in transmitting, or rather working from, the basis and context of an incarnational theology (a theology of nature and grace, of creation and incarnation) that is still unfamiliar to many Catholic/Christian believers. (There are, of course, many other reasons for today's challenges to the message of our pastoral workers.) The intention in this section is to accept the suggestion of OTWTL to explore paths and possibilities for growth and discovery.

The challenges are not totally new.

It is consoling to realise that such challenges are not totally new. In a sense, it has ever been so. St Anselm's famous dictum, *fides quaerens intellectum*, acknowledges the continual search for an accurate understanding of what we believe, and for appropriate ways of sharing that belief. The attuning of God's Word to the human ear will always occur in the context of specific settings of time and space. The history of Christianity contains innumerable accounts of such ultimately graced moments of conflict, encounter and progress. The early disputes in Jerusalem, the councils of the church, the great debates, the challenges to missionary work all over the world, are all testaments to that painful and purifying interface when Christianity encounters unfamiliar crises and opportunities for the translation and transmission of its good news. What is different about the current set of challenges is its suddenness on the one hand, and, on the other, our classic unreadiness for its now-relentless appearance. 'The church always arrives on the scene,' the jibe goes, 'but always a little breathless and a little late!'

How do we hold fast to our hard-won truth and tradition while encountering 'the stranger' in the guise of diverse races, cultures, religions, in a postmodern world? As with every such encounter with 'the other', there are both dangers and opportunities. The dangers are many and

serious. They are well chronicled by our recent popes. It would be fool-
ish to underestimate the grip that postmodernism has on today's world
and, indeed, we would do well to search our own hearts for its undoubted
presence within them. Pope John Paul II was of the opinion that eternal
truths make no sense to a postmodern mindset.

Nevertheless, this section is about discussing the possibilities of some
positive dimensions in our Catholic awareness of, and response to, the
phenomena of religious pluralism and postmodernism. To be sure, the
terrorism of religious extremists and the social injustice and environmental irresponsibility of a galloping consumerism will always fly in the
face of human striving for a better world. As Catholics, however, while
we are hopefully well aware of the destructive potential of these particular phenomena, we are often guilty of excessively negative attitudes in
the face of the general, current challenge of postmodernism.

These attitudes include the denial of this new reality, an increase of the
familiar 'head in the sand' syndrome, or a fundamentalist and aggressive
'circling of the wagons' in the face of a perceived attack. Then there are
those who 'leave it all to God' and wait for a miracle. Or their secret goal
in seeking to encounter the 'strangers' may be to baptise them! So, while
aspects of postmodernity are arrogantly strangling humane efforts
towards justice and peace, we can ask whether other dimensions of it
can be regarded as 'a cultural wavelength' in which, through critical
reflection, faith can grow stronger and be more credible today.[1] Among
the opportunities is the need for a certain self-assessment about our
basic truth each time an unfamiliar situation arises. *Ecclesia semper
reformanda*. In times of crisis we are drawn to a deeper awareness and
understanding of our own beliefs.

Developing Doctrines

'If the only faith we know is our own, then we do not even know that',
Bishop Newbigin famously held. Our fragmented understanding of the
divine is enriched and enlightened by the sharing of our insights and
stories with others in trust and love. Also, in honest dialogue with other
faiths, the inadequacy of any one set of propositions to encapsulate the
God of Infinite Mystery is revealed. There is, as we have already
touched upon, a temptation for Christians to identify faith with doctrines. No matter how thoroughly honed and revered these may be, they
will never capture the fullness of God's life and action. No amount of
adding up of beliefs or doctrines can ever equal faith. They will always
be subordinate to, and answerable to, the transcendent reality of God.

As Catholics we are often guilty of excessively negative attitudes in the face of the challenge of post-modernism.

In his *The Survival of Dogma*, Cardinal Avery Dulles insists that dogmas are 'entry-points' into the mysteries of faith and are not exhaustive descriptions of their meaning. Perhaps nobody protected this principle more adequately than Cardinal John Henry Newman did in his writings, and especially in *Development of Doctrine* where he was always on the look-out for new lines of doctrinal development so as to tap into the greater mystery that the doctrines protected and served.

Demonising postmodernism is not the appropriate response from a mature Christianity.

Demonising postmodernism is not the appropriate response from a mature Christianity. Hand in hand with the different discourses and secular dynamics of a complicated world reality, there is, too, a desire for wholeness and renewal, a search for meaning in a fragmented culture, for a point of trust in a disconnected society. There is a hidden groping towards some kind of 'common good'. OTWTL points out that the church needs to do some hard thinking in order to build a bridge and to formulate a language which will engage contemporary culture in a dialogue, and convince it of the truth of what it believes and proclaims.

The meeting-place for this dialogue forms, and is formed by, a rich sense of humanity (and humility) on the part of both partners in the dialogue. After all, the various guises of modernity and postmodernity cannot be avoided since they are found in our own mindset. They form part of our own mental constructs and evoke different reactions within ourselves.

> Ultimately, what we are seeking is not safety but truth. And truth cannot deceive. But when we label 'truth' too soon we deny its divine origin.

Humbly and confidently we enter, with discernment and friendship, into the courageous conversation.

For Thomas Aquinas, the doctrines of faith were signposts to mystery, not ends in themselves. All our best thinkers welcomed the challenges and opportunities for staying open to new possibilities for as long as possible. Truth is a mystery to be reverently searched for; it is not a possession to be jealously guarded and enforced. Little is gained from polarising issues too soon. Where both sides have only a veiled contempt for one another (as is often the case), then there will be no growing. Humbly and confidently we enter, with discernment and friendship, into the courageous conversation. We all have a wonderful story to tell.

A 'Catholic modernity' is described as 'an alternative vision of the modern age, understanding reality as bathed in grace, and so intrinsically open to God. Consequently, through this sacramental vision of reality, human existence is understood in the light of a Christian humanism, understanding the human as an image of God.'[2] Has Catholic culture the power to transform contemporary culture where it is weakest, catching both readjusted cultures up into God's plan of salvation for all humanity? 'If modernity seeks to be self-grounding, Vatican II seeks to demonstrate how it can be grounded in the transcendent in such a way that its fundamental values are not lost but more completely expressed and secured.'[3]

Professor Nicholas Boyle, quoted in a *Tablet* article (2006), holds that 'the centrality of the human is the distinguishing feature of the Christian religion and the reason why it can properly be called the original humanism ... In so far as it is humanist, Christianity can recognise the humanism of other religions, and the extent to which their adherents know that the ultimate reality is known through human being, human love and self-sacrifice.' (See also 'The state we are in' by Nicholas Boyle, *The Tablet* 19 April 2008.)

If we speak about the possibility of a mutual dialogue then we, in turn, are called to listen out for opportunities for the purification and enrichment of Catholicism in the encounter with the postmodern world and by its critique of our belief-system. One of the spin-offs from such a scrutiny, according to theologian Stanley Grenz, is a potential loosening up of a Catholic inflexibility about religious knowledge, education and behaviour, bringing in a readiness to explore the boundaries with a little more enthusiasm.

> Postmodern critique, he holds, can be helpful in achieving a 'post-dualistic' gospel; that is, one in which artificial dichotomies such as that between 'soul' and' body', 'nature' and 'grace', can be overcome with a deeper sense of holistic salvation that is inclusive and relational, that holds together not only the 'intellectual-rational' features of our humanity, but also the 'emotive-affective' aspects as well. Such a critique can only contribute positive clues, the evangelical Grenz believes, for re-casting and re-shaping the mission of the church to spread the gospel.

In his *Theological Education in a Postmodern Era*, Dr J. J. McCarthy praises the work of Thomas Guarino, a Catholic theologian, in examining the pros and cons of the Christian encounter with postmodernism. He suggests that postmodern concerns about the irreducibility of the 'Other' are indeed valuable reminders that theological language can never do justice to God. The long apophatic tradition of theological discourse that emphasises the *via negativa* is reflected in the work of the Cappadocian Fathers, especially Gregory Nazianzen, and in the work of Thomas Aquinas.

Mutual Respect – spirituality, humility, courage, vision

Another precarious but possibly vital 'bridge of meeting' between Christianity and both other faiths and the postmodern reality, is 'spirituality'. The quest for spirituality, whether as a member of a faith-community or as a postmodern seeker, is at least a possible site for dialogue. Spirituality can transcend both the institutional religions of the world, and the rejection of such religions by a pluralistic postmodernity. Where world faiths are concerned, there is a remarkable similarity in the mystical, spiritual heart of each of them.

Spirituality can transcend both the institutional religions of the world, and the rejection of such religions by a pluralistic postmodernity.

A theology of nature and grace goes a long way towards explaining why this is so. Here we find potential for the beginning of an ecumenical renewal. But also, though many may well deny it, the human hearts of the postmodernists are *naturaliter religiosa*, innately religious. The quest for spirituality goes some way towards answering the existential questions of purpose and identity which they are asking. And while the reluctant postmodern admission of interest in spirituality is often more about the arcane, the occult in religious phenomena and New Age pantheism, nevertheless, perhaps a real possibility is opened up there for mutual interest and understanding.

Because, according to George Lotter and Glendon Thompson in their *Challenges and Opportunities of Postmodernism for the Church*, Christianity is 'awash with new and divergent theologies', then there are bound to be opportunities for much mutually enriching conversation about a whole range of issues that would be familiar to most thinking seekers after truth; from the extremes of dogmatism, on the one hand, to those of utter nihilism, on the other. There is a whole arena of potential debate about 'the spiritual' at that explosive point where Christian faith meets postmodern conviction. Because such committed postmodern conviction is, from the Christian point of view, to some extent at least the creative work of God in human beings, then there is no need to be afraid of it. Truth is not going to damage itself.

Truth is not going to damage itself.

McCarthy ends his essay on an upbeat note: 'I have come to the conclusion,' he writes, 'that postmodern thinkers have not brought an end to philosophy or theology. The image that comes to mind is this: at the airport we are accustomed to rigorous screening of our luggage. Postmodern thinkers serve as critical reviewers of our intellectual 'luggage', including our theological traditions. In that capacity, they serve a useful function of detecting possible distortions or difficulties in the conceptual apparatus of our traditions, but their particular screens or filters are themselves subject to critical assessment. To the extent that good, critical questions identify "problems" in the luggage, they are helpful. But good screening does not eliminate the luggage, nor does it prevent the luggage from reaching its destination. Embedded within these critiques or screens is the drive for totality, completion and wholeness that is never an achieved, once-for-all artifact, but rather an ongoing process of discovery.'[4]

Many informed commentators on this issue hold, with McCarthy, that we do not have to soft-pedal the intensity of our faith, or lose our own soul, in the mutual examination we are discussing. To the extent that engagement with postmodern currents galvanises and energises our capacity to meet the needs of the church as it faces dialogue with the great religions of the world, and the enormous challenges of a planet that is becoming more and not less connected, globally and across cultures, then it continues to provide a useful tool for a more informed, intelligent and measured way of doing God's work.

At the very least, we can meet our brothers and sisters from other faiths on equal ground as long as we do so reverently, honouring what they believe as we honour our own commitments to Christianity, leaving the fruits of such an embrace to God. We can also stand our ground with postmodernity as we meet, perhaps on a common footing, namely in the commitment so dear to postmodern thinkers, that we 'keep the conversation going.'

After all, our true role, standing humbly before the Great Mystery, is that of listening to the word, ever prepared to learn just a little more in the many classrooms of the religions of life. Nicholas Lash provides a timely reminder.

> 'Thus it is that the great religions of the world function as schools in which people learn that there is no one feature of the world – no nation, institution, person, text, idea, ambition – that is, quite simply, sacred ... It is within the (whole) world, in all of the world, in all we think and do and say and see, achieve and suffer, and by no means only in some small margin of the world which people these days call "religion", that we are required to be attentive to the promptings of the Spirit, responsive to the breath of God.'[5]

Is there a loss of nerve in our churches at the moment? Why do we find it hard to look outwards with anticipation and welcome at the speed of progress and the wonder of human ingenuity? There is an atmosphere of anxiety in the life of the church, a feeling of insecurity and hesitation. It makes us perceive what is different as threat rather than gift. We find

What is needed to be true to the freedom of God in creating and in becoming human, is a reclaiming of our own mystical imagination.

the 'stranger', the 'other', intimidating rather than worthy of service. What is needed to be true to the freedom of God in creating and in becoming human, is a reclaiming of our own mystical imagination. Otherwise we tend to limit God in the most fearful of ways. We allow God only the same attitudes and characteristics as we can muster up in ourselves. Our limitations become God's. We forget that God is infinitely beyond anything we can conjure up and that this God has placed a divine creativity and longing in every human heart.

John Paul II reminded us of this in his Christmas homily at the beginning of the new millennium when he spoke about '... the immortal genius of Michelangelo portrayed on the ceiling of the Sistine Chapel, the moment when God the Father communicated the gift of life to the first man and made him "a living being". Between the finger of God and the finger of man stretching out to each other and almost touching, there seems to leap an invisible spark: God communicates to man a tremor of his own life, creating him in his image and likeness. That divine breath is the origin of the unique dignity of every human being, of humanity's boundless yearning for the infinite.'

These words of our late pope offer us food for thought, especially when it comes to meeting the challenge of introducing a more human-centred theology to teachers and catechists who are familiar only with a sin/redemption emphasis (Part Two). Springing from an often dubious theology of original sin, this centuries-old exposure to an exclusive atonement-type understanding of Christ's life and death has had an enormous effect on our teaching and preaching about our attitude to a threatening world. What is so timely and promising about OTWTL is its espousal of a divine-human story that emphasises God's delight in creation and incarnation; a story that restores a pride and a beauty to the world and to humanity; a story whose faint echo, already and always in our hearts, is getting stronger by the day during these early years of a new millennium.

This emerging good news is again emphasised through the OTWTL authors' efforts to release the glorious promise of Vatican II, to nurture the belated flowering of that anticipated springtime so long in its coming. *Gaudium et spes* explains that in the past we over-emphasised the notion of two different worlds, one sacred, one profane. The image that this notion suggests is that of a two-storey house, where the secular and the sacred are on separate levels, where grace impacts on nature but never really belongs to it, enhances or transforms it. What we call the Catholic imagination needs to be swiftly 're-evangelised' for this dualism to be transcended. Knowingly or not, from its inmost roots, the world is constantly seized by divine self-communication. God's grace is everywhere present as an abiding determinant of the human spirit.

Unfamiliar Growing Places

Over ten years ago the Jesuit General Congregation, in *Our Mission and Culture*, addressed the question about what postmodernity, with its 'impulse to disbelief', implies for Christian doctrine and practice. While clearly acknowledging that the gospel, at least in its traditional language and institutions, is swiftly losing credibility, the document sees the post-modern phenomenon as a time of useful challenge and potential purific-ation. Postmodern concerns for the social, bodily rooting of our knowl-edge, and for ecological and environmental values, may be taken as pointers towards Christ and the Spirit.[6]

> The postmodern insistence on finding meaning 'within the very structure of human, embodied experience' converges with Christian belief in the incarnation: similarly, the commitment to the natural, cosmic order connects with Christian discourse about the Holy Spirit.

For example, even though a thoroughly secular postmodernity would regard the pain of the world as meaningless in a nihilistic kind of hope-lessness, nevertheless there are indications in its literature that a real but wholesome humanism is concerned and compassionate about the mys-tery of universal suffering. One can detect an openness to all that deep-ens our understanding of the struggle of a broken humanity. 'From the beginning till now the entire creation has been groaning in one great act of giving birth, and not only creation but all of us too groan inwardly as we wait for our bodies to be set free.' (Rom 8:22)

If crises carry opportunities for transcendence, where else do we look for transforming seeds within the complicated and critical interface between current and ambiguous trends of pluralism in society on the one hand, and the age-old traditions and certainties of the churches on the other? Can an appropriate, and even necessary, kind of development arise from postmodernism's sceptical subversion of religious languages and cultures, making us look again at our understanding of God's inscrutable mysteriousness and God's unknowable otherness?

Postmodernism is uneasy with all certainties, especially scientific and religious ones. There is no place for 'grand narratives' in a worldview that is associated with unpredictability and provisionality. In such a mind-set, the notion of a personably knowable God is regarded with open suspicion. Yet the readiness to admit to a transcendent horizon, to a commitment to pursue the question of how to know the other *as the other*, is ready ground for mutual exploring. To repeat, maybe we should be persuaded to recover the tradition of absence, of unknowing – the apophatic way, the *via negativa* already referred to.

Thomas Aquinas held that we can know almost nothing of a God who is radically different from any premise we can posit of that God. Writing about this tradition, Philip Endean SJ explains that 'it represents a disciplined awareness, on the basis of the revelation we have, that God is inexhaustible mystery.

> To know that one does not know the mystery of God, to know that one can only wonder at and about it, is nevertheless an important form of knowledge, and indeed, the only true knowledge of the God available to us. If postmodernism strengthens our openness to accepting this kind of knowledge for what it is – no more, no less – its contribution to Christian spirituality can be very great.'[7]

If we persist in our belief in the God of Jesus rather than the God of the philosophers, if we trust that the God who made all things is vibrantly alive in postmodern people living in a postmodern world, and if we recover, and optimistically exercise the Catholic sacramental imagination in a rather unpromising contemporary situation, then maybe we are at the threshold of an unexpected breakthrough.

If this breakthrough is to happen, if we are ever to respond to a beckoning God's invitation to 'launch out into the deep' at many levels, then a time of humble, open contemplation on our part will be a first requirement. The so-called Godless society may turn out to be a *milieu divin* after all. 'The sense of absurdity which is another characteristic of our situation, may well be more in tune with the logic of this God (of Jesus), whose wisdom and power seem like foolishness and powerlessness to human understanding, than is traditional theology's reliance on reason and analogy.'[8]

A theology of nature and grace will relish the opportunity of validating its claims in a postmodern world. It would not be the first time that the incarnate God found new self-expression in a Bethlehem place of confusion and contradiction. It is often precisely where absurdity and disillusionment abound that the divine presence is revealed in the most unexpected ways. Despite its confident 'deconstruction' of previous ways of thinking, talking and feeling, there are postmodern writers who will admit to a prevailing sense of vulnerability in their 'philosophies' of life. In Christian terms, this awareness is nearly always a near-occasion for grace to build on.

Listening, openness, contemplation

Vulnerability and uncertainty carry a resonance of openness. Where there is openness there is an immense reason for hope. What is now waiting to be explored is the possibility of a postmodern spirituality, an approach to contemporary realities where the main tenets, energies and explorations of postmodernism are welcomed and respected. Careless rejection only leads to alienation. The possibility of mutual growth in wisdom and compassion, of healing and redemption, is pushed even further away. A postmodern spirituality would be more humble, less sure, more receptive. It would carry overtones of mysticism, that under-rated yet dynamic dimension of current Christianity. The mystical trad-ition is renowned for its openness to mystery, its exploration into the unknown, its discomfort with final definitions or dogmas. Meister Eckhart's words 'I pray to God to rid me of God' might find a listening ear among today's postmodernists!

A postmodern spirituality would be more humble, less sure, more receptive.

They might listen, also, to a spirituality that is no longer preoccupied with individual salvation from a dangerous world. There is a Christian communitarian spirituality which is committed to integrating religion with real life, and which, in today's clash of cultures, enables incultur-ation as the essential condition of a commitment to liberation. Rafael Esteban writes: 'Inculturation demands a listening to the Spirit that works in all human hearts and cultures, respecting it and appreciating it, but also a boldness which can denounce the narrowness and dehuman-ising aspects of all cultures while letting those cultures challenge their own dia-bolic (divisive) sides. Liberation demands a total commitment to freedom, to life and peace, together with the readiness to endure oppressive structures while denouncing them in the name of the king-dom. This spirituality is essentially a "political" spirituality, because it is rooted in the reality of people's needs.'[9]

Our past teaches us that the future must remain unpredictable. In gen-eral terms, then, what would a concept of spirituality, or of evangelising look like in a postmodern age? John O'Donoghue believes that much of the language of religion is caught in a time-warp. It attempts to speak with the voice of a vanished age to a fragmented culture that has out-grown it. Far from being an imposition of the gospel on people, or the awakening of their spiritual sense so as to institutionalise it, evangelis-ation touches the deepest origin, memory, identity and destiny of the human individual and of communities.

John O'Donoghue believes that much of the language of religion is caught in a time-warp. It attempts to speak with the voice of a vanished age to a fragmented culture that has outgrown it.

'This news', he writes, 'comes from the very well of life itself. It encour-ages life to celebrate and honour all its possibilities and risks. This is the news that life itself is the primal sacrament; that life is the home of the eternal, albeit in veiled form; that the life of each person is a sacrament, wherein the eternal seeks to become visible and active; that each individual is chosen for a creative destiny in this world; that each one incarnates a different dimension of God; that at death life is not ended, but elevated and transfigured into another form; that we are not outside, but within, God.'[10]

There is an inbuilt flexibility and adaptability to the theology of nature and grace that underpins our hope for an enriched and fulfilling approach to teaching and catechising. Vincent Donovan reminded us many years ago, we do not bring God to people. 'We awaken the presence of God in them. This is the heart of the spiritual journey, to bring that presence to awareness. This is a delicate and sensitive work. Awareness cannot be forced; it can only be awakened.'[11] A theology of nature and grace never loses touch with the imagination nor with the central place of experience; it honours the life-giving memory of what God has done for us in the past; it is sensitive to the uses of language in a pluralist society; it sees the relief of the poverty and pain of the world as its main concern; it remains open to the mystical wisdom that ultimately it is here that all things and peoples are revealed as belonging together.

The universal is found in the particular. We have seen that at the core of Karl Rahner's incarnational theology is the conviction that God's transcendental self-communication is already intrinsic to the concrete world. Having spent years exploring this mystery, he adds two very helpful observations. One has to do with the central place of contemplation in all our work. 'All the societal supports of religion are collapsing in this secularised and pluralistic society. If, nonetheless, there is to be really Christian spirituality, it cannot be kept alive and healthy by external helps, not even those which the church offers, even of a sacramental kind ... but only through ultimate immediate encounter between the individual and God.'[12] The universal is found in the particular.

The second observation carries a healthy reminder for those who insist that we already have all the doctrinal answers we need to face the future, or who strive to move too quickly to a new, inspired theology that anticipates and copes with the challenges of a postmodern world. 'A theology that wishes to answer all questions clearly and thoroughly is guaranteed to miss its proper object.'[13] Commenting on these consoling words, theologian Dermot Lane reminds us that those who speak with dogmatic certainty and excessive clarity have lost sight of the subject of theology.[14] Von Balthasar holds that 'we can only "do theology" on our knees'.

Missionaries within Secularity

The Jesuits are not the only ones to relish the current encounter with religions and cultures in a postmodern era. A few years ago the Oblates of Mary Immaculate (OMI) sponsored a symposium at St Paul University, Ottawa, to look at the complexities of being missionary within the culture of postmodernism. They invited a mixed group of experienced people to reach some 'missiological principles' for the future. Among them were John Shea, Richard Rohr and Ronald Rolheiser. Here are 10 of their reflections:

- We are at a new place today in terms of the faith. Adaptation of what worked in the past may not be enough. We need to re-inflame the romantic imagination within Christianity.

- Secularity is not the enemy. Secularity is our own child, sprung from Judeo-Christian roots. Like any adolescent child, its not bad, just unfinished. The 'soil' of secularity is defined by Jesus in the parable of the Sower. The fact that some ground is hostile or indifferent is no excuse for stopping sowing.

- Spirituality is people's birthright. The secular culture hungers for spirituality, but is largely spiritually illiterate. People go where they get fed.

- We must seek to recover the heart of our tradition, beyond its encrusted accretions, and then add our own passion to that heart. We must work at finding our own faith-voice and then speak in an invitational way. Part of this must be a profound ascesis of listening.

- A place of contact with the postmodern world could be the fertile image of Christ as the *kenosis* of God. In his self-emptying, he reveals a God without pretence, a God of pure invitation, non-violence and vulnerability; a God who accepts the provisionality of everything. Jesus' essential message is a universal message.

- Given this self-emptying God, we might remember that sharing the mission of Christ does not always mean using religious language. It is a time for finding other, more effective forms of transmission.

- As a faith community we are in exile from the power, possessiveness and prestige of the past. But all transformation happens in exile because only then can God get at us. We need to stay with the pain, the exile, the *kenosis*, and hold the tension long enough until it changes us.

- There are four aspects of the church that people still do accept: the church as an agency to serve the poor, the church as delivering the rites of passage, the church as a voice within ethical discourse, and the church as a 'beautiful heritage'. We are more than those dimensions. But, as well as a new language, do we need new 'missiological' structures, new 'ecclesial houses', beyond the parish, to supplement current pastoral possibilities?

- Part of evangelisation is the movement to eliminate poverty. If we want to work at home and abroad for this to happen, we must free ourselves from too much reliance on dogma, and rely more on human solidarity.

- We need to accept the broad solid human foundations for moral progress within our culture, and widen the pool of sincere people who form one body, to work for a better world. Excessive stress on religious and denominational identification can narrow that body. Inter-religious dialogue must lead back to a common humanity. We need to commit ourselves not just to the baptised but to all people of sincerity and good will. (Compiled by Ronald Rolheiser)

'In brief,' Dermot Lane writes, 'Christian faith will have to present itself as intrinsic to the human condition and not outside it, as apologetic and not authoritarian, as ecumenical and not sectarian, as inter-religious and not exclusive, as affectively reasonable and not coldly rational. Such qualities and characteristics of Christian faith are an intrinsic part of the dynamism of the mystery of Jesus Christ as the eternal Word and Wisdom of God made flesh in history.'[15]

Summary

The scandal of particularity – revelation can happen only in the setting of today's world, in the particular circumstances of the here and now.

There are hidden opportunities for dialogue within a pluralist, postmodern world. Its relativism is not always an evil thing. Without courage and trust there will be no true progress, no healing growth.

What we are seeking is not safety but truth. And truth does not work against itself. Some postmodern concerns can be seen as pointers towards gospel values.

The encounter with the 'other' draws us to a deeper awareness and purification of our own beliefs.

A theology of nature and grace is a common ground for dialogue with other faiths and cultures in a postmodern world.

The Catholic culture has the power to transform contemporary culture where it is weakest.

But first it needs to formulate a language which will engage other cultures in a dialogue with the church.

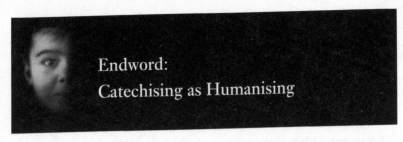

Endword:
Catechising as Humanising

In general, this Endword is a brief recapitulation and summary of some of the main themes running through *Begin with the Heart*. It repeats a few significant observations and quotations to remind us of the central place of a theology of nature and grace in our work. As OTWTL emphasises, theology influences the aims, content and language of the way we evangelise, teach, preach and celebrate liturgy. This section recalls the Project's main theme about the central place of humanity in our faith story. It does this by contrasting, under the headings of theology, evangelisation, liturgy and language, two occasionally differing approaches to the holy work of 'handing on the faith'. It tries to indicate how, when they are at their best, these approaches need each other so as to be true to the gospel.

Suppose, after a conversation with one of the women that came to talk to him, Jesus was asked about the precise nature of what went on between them. Was it adult education or formation, evangelisation or pre-evangelisation, catechesis or pre-catechesis? How amazed he would be. He might just reply, 'Oh no; it was nothing like that. We were just having a heart-to-heart chat. Lovely person. She made me feel better. We've arranged to meet again.' More at home with church-speak, we are often confused by simple, straightforward communication!

When it comes to a many-faceted term such as 'catechesis' or 'evangelisation' have we complicated things too much for people? Does friendship and intimacy with the Risen Christ not transcend all such mental divisions and distinctions? To be sure, all of these well-defined delineations and emphases have their place. They sometimes clarify things. But for ordinary souls is there a simpler way of talking about loving God or Jesus? Where 'heart speaks to heart' the head does not always need to dominate. Real love has its own self-expression. Maybe it is time to recover the language of love in the work of education.

Maybe it is time to recover the language of love in the work of education.

After nearly half a century trying to teach, preach, evangelise and cate-chise, I sometimes wonder whether we get lost too easily in the persist-ent search for rational clarity; whether we confuse religious knowledge (and religious behaviour) with a heart-felt sense of belonging to God; whether we lose sight of falling in love with God in pursuit of a more doctrinally explicit creed of beliefs. Is there a great danger of missing the stunning message of the incarnation, and its implications for our humanity, through insisting too much on a prescribed progression through pre-arranged hoops and sequential stages of initiation? Evangelisation will always be grounded in the simplicity and profundity of the way human hearts touch each other.

Or we may ask whether too much emphasis can be placed on an overly 'evangelical-type' of Jesus-worship that seems to be strangely silent about a surrender of our hearts to God our Saviour, and to the practical building up of the kingdom of 'a God of all names'? There is a growing fund-amentalism within Christianity that is popular and powerful. Christian educ-ation can be seen as a way of liberating people from such crusading fund-amentalism into the glorious, human freedom of being children of God.

Put another way, what actually is the experience of a relationship with the person of Jesus? Is it not more than the adoration and worship of him, the knowledge about him, the creeds of the churches? Has it not more to do with the following of him, acquiring the mind and vision of him, sharing the passion of his overflowing heart and of his wounded body, and doing what he asked us to do?' Surely it can be no other than living and believing the sacramental vision of our transformed human-ity in Christ, and consequently, our new empowerment to change the world so beloved of his Father?

In 2006 the Jesuits celebrated major anniversaries of their three founders. Michael Holman, their Provincial Superior, has written about the way they endeavoured to spread the Word. Having commented on the limited success of many recent attempts to evangelise, he suggests that we learn something from the approach of these pioneering men. They held that the secularism of their time was such 'that it could not be met by argument, only by an experience of Christ. Theirs was a per-sonal approach that began with a conversation. It was never a matter of imposing Christ but of recommending him, proposing him as attractive because, first and foremost, he was supremely attractive to them. They managed to do what we find it hard to do: they evangelised the whole person, *spiritu, corde, practice* – in the spirit, from the heart, practically.' (See 'St Francis Xavier and Today's Mission in Europe' by Michael Holman in *The Tablet*, 1 December 2006).

There are many well-meaning but misleading emphases in our current approaches to evangelisation that obscure the powerful simplicity of the message of Jesus – a message that has to do with the purifying and completing of our humanity, with lives given over entirely to Christ. As we continue to devote ourselves to the things of God, perennially committed to spreading the word and building the Reign, is there a place for some spring-cleaning to clear away unnecessary and distracting verbiage?

There are many well-meaning but misleading emphases in our current approaches to evangelisation.

There is a story about Vince Lombardi, the famous American football coach. His team had plummeted from the top of the league. The previous season they had dazzled the country with the magic and sophistication of their passing strategies, their scoring techniques, their winning ways. This year they had lost the plot completely. He called them together and settled them down. 'We need to dismantle all the unnecessary clutter of yesterday.' he said to them. 'Here are the basics. This thing in my hand is called a football. And these are your legs and arms. Now our aim is to get that ball, using your legs and arms, in spite of those who will try to stop us, from one end of the field to the other.'

Two Theologies

For those who wish to embark on such an exercise of simplification, of clarifying the central aims of our various ministries, of trying to focus again on the heart of the mission and vision of Jesus, there are many starting-points. For now, out of many possibilities, we look at four dimensions of such work, offering a few free-flowing reflections on each – theology, evangelisation, liturgy, and language. The aim is to show that these aspects of our faith, and for that matter, all the dimensions of Catholic education and catechesis, are not ends in themselves (important as this outcome may be in other more cerebral contexts) but thresholds into the unique Christian revelation that we are loved intensely by a God who became human so as to convince us of that life-changing truth.

Unpopular and inaccessible as many aspects of theology may be – and mainly because they mostly leave our needy lives untouched – it is important to remember that all our efforts to grow closer to God through prayer and the sacraments, and all our efforts to teach, preach and catechise, are shaped and nourished by some theology or other. When that theology is all about sin and redemption, then our relationship with God will be deeply affected by how shameful we are for somehow being part of the original sin that forced God to become one of us.

And, because of that, for causing the crucifixion of Jesus. Our catechesis, our liturgy, our teaching and preaching, our hymns and our public prayers, will then be bound to carry this heavy shadow – the shadow of fear, unworthiness, guilt. Many would hold that such is the way it still is.

When, however, the theology that inspires us is coloured and textured by a love-story of God's utter delight in creating and saving us, in becoming one of us, and in finding divine happiness by living intimately with us now, our prayers, celebrations, evangelising and homilies will carry an entirely different energy and intimacy. Unlike the dualistic, divisive impact of doctrines that emphasise our sinfulness and unworthiness alone, the reassurance that we are also already shining with the presence of a God who is utterly at home in us and with us is positively transforming for human beings.

The reassurance that we are also already shining with the presence of a God who is utterly at home in us and with us is positively transforming for human beings.

This latter doctrinal stance springs from what we have been calling a theology of nature and grace. Full of intense compassion, God wished to create out of pure love, and then, in time, to *become* that creation. That becoming happened in Jesus Christ. In him it was revealed that God's heart beats in all our hearts, that all our bodies are temples of the Holy Spirit, and that every creature is a divine work of art. Revelation (and all forms of Christian education) is about the unbelievable possibilities of humanity, graced at its centre from the very beginning. It is about God's desire to be known and loved in the humanity of Jesus Christ. It is about God's delight in being visible and tangible in human form.

> It is very important, we noted, to clarify the awful reality of original sin in each one of us personally, and in humanity as a whole. To be deeply flawed, and attracted towards sin, is part of the definition of being human. And that is why we sorely need saving from self-destruction. We do terrible things to each other as individuals and as nations. Our theology is a theology of redemption. We must make no mistake about that. What is important to remember, however, is that there is more to the story than a divine rescue-operation. The original revelation is of a God who was moved to create out of intense love, to become a part of that creation, to die out of love for us, and to remain with us forever in our deepest hearts. A theology of sin and redemption needs the wider horizon of a theology of nature and grace to reveal its true context and meaning.

In the beautiful theology of creation and incarnation, of nature and grace, the fleshing of God has revealed, once and for all, what it means to be truly human. We achieve our true humanity, not by running away from the world and its joys and pleasures, or by turning our backs on it in fear or doubt. Christ does not reveal what it is to be divine but what it is to be human. It is often said that we are not human beings trying to become spiritual. We are spiritual beings trying to become truly human. That our often-faint God-likeness might become purified, intensified and completed in us, is the purpose of creation and incarnation. It is also the point and purpose of our catechising and preaching.

This completion, this transformation is not something added on from the outside, so to speak, to our 'mere' human nature – a kind of divine layer on top of our ordinary humanity. It is rather the revelation of the intrinsic meaning of our very lives. The graced unfolding of our lives is God's dream within us becoming true. The Second Vatican Council was so clear about all of this. Since God desired from the very beginning to become human, the incarnation reveals the meaning of the humanity of all of us. And that is that we are all sacraments of God's love. The VaticanII document *The Church in the Modern World* reminds us that because Jesus 'worked with human hands, thought with a human mind, acted by human choice, and loved with a human heart' we are all ordained to share in that same grounded priestliness. (par 22)

We are all sacraments of God's love.

There is a lift and a depth about a theology of nature and grace. It discerns the free movement of the Holy Spirit wherever people are committed to genuine human values and humanitarian pursuits. It identifies the longing for God in all human longing. It sees God's spirit ranging across the whole spectrum of creation, of history and of individual experiences in ways far beyond the constricted and limited places, people and things to which many of our textbook theologies, catechisms and homiletic suggestions would restrict it. It takes its shape and texture from the passion of Jesus for making possible for everybody, the actual here-and-now experience of the abundant life. And whatever we may mean by catechesis or evangelisation, the moment it loses that life-giving empowerment as its main thrust, then it has lost everything.

Moral theologian and parish priest Fr Kevin Kelly has written: 'Evangelisation is really about something very simple, wonderful and exciting. It is about being truly human, each in our own unique way, and thus translating and interpreting God's love story in the language of our modern age – and so helping people read that same story in the wonder of their own being and even in the ambiguity of their lives.'

Two Approaches to Evangelisation and Catechesis

Such an earthy, healthy theology is the reason why there should be something instantly recognisable as good news whenever we are engaged in evangelising, catechising or spiritually forming those we serve – as there was in the life and relationships of Jesus. The whole point of his coming was to bring an abundance to people's lives by his very presence – a presence that healed and captured hearts and minds and bodies in a way that arguments and progressive stages of knowledge, as the early missionaries realised, never could.

Jesus did not measure his friendship, or the deepening trust of his disciples, or the emotional bonds within his followers, in holy steps and compartmentalised progressions. Living relationships are not like that. They do not subject themselves to analysis as worked-out theories do. People were simply drawn to his company, attracted by his humanity. Because they did not feel judged, their hearts expanded in his presence. The best in them was touched even as the worst in them was understood. You could say that they felt so good about themselves just by being around him, by being loved by him. When that central excitement is withdrawn, denied or lost from the very core of the process of evangelisation, or catechesis, or preaching, then, whatever else we may think we are doing, we are not presenting the human Christ as he was; we are not telling the whole truth about the Christian story.

'Handing on the Faith' is not primarily about a mental assent to sets of beliefs, or about telling people things that are completely new and essentially different, adding to their knowledge, coming to them from the outside, so to speak.

> It is more about convincing them of something they already suspect, of assuring them that the faint dream they carry is, in fact, true, and that the intuitions of their heart about the mystery of their being, are confirmed and guaranteed by Jesus Christ.

It is true to say that people's own hearts recognise, and delight in, and are transformed by, the authentic validity of such evangelisation.

There is no denying the reality of this kind of life-transforming good news. Only those who are deeply moved themselves by it can ever be true teachers and facilitators of the 'two-edged sword' that reaches to our inmost places. Christian leaders today repeatedly call for more fire and vision in those who are privileged to be part of the various pastoral ministries in the churches.

A whole-hearted commitment to evangelisation, religious education and preaching would suggest some of the following aims as central summaries of that passionate work of pastoral faith-education:

- Jesus is revealed as the language, the body-language, the human body of God. When God enters our space and time, our loving Creator emerges in the person and personality of Jesus. It follows that all human beings, then, without exception, are God's language too. And it is God's delight to be dwelling within us. A huge dimension of our holy work is to keep telling this astonishing story in the music, dance and poetry of a living sharing, in the revealing to people the truth about their own divine identity, in telling them who they really are.

- How to convince people that they are unconditionally loved by a God who is so delighted to be intimately one with them? It takes a huge paradigm shift in our innermost spirit to transcend the negativity and dualism of so much of our inherited misunderstanding of ecclesiastical laws and teachings. Many of us need a deep conversion before we can reach into, and experience, the freedom of the daughters and sons of God. The fragility and tenderness of God's desire for our total trust and surrender have been lost in translation and interpretation.

- The Good News reaches in to the demonic powers within us, and within our society and world, so that we can name and dismantle those dark spirits, finding a new courage, a new heart, to continue on, no matter what. Jesus saved people's lives by filling them with redemptive hope. The first concern of Jesus was to set people free from their despair and their fears, to bring the light of joy into their daily lives, to enable them to live a more abundant life in the here and now. Persistent images from the past of a hard God still make it so difficult for us to trust ourselves to the personal, human, constant and unconditional divine love revealed in Jesus.

- Central to any context for such a liberating, comforting and life-giving understanding of Revelation is the humanity of Jesus. Any true Christian formation can ever only draw its wisdom, its justification and its never-ending inspiration and nourishment from that first principle of incarnation – the humanity of God as personified in Jesus. This is the humanity through which we are saved; the humanity that attracted people to follow Jesus, forming his first community of faith; the humanity that people fell in love with, and their lives were changed forever. It was an 'ordinary' humanity in which he suffered much, lived life to the hilt, lost his good name, felt abandoned by his father, confronted and redeemed his darkness. This was the

kind of needy and authentic humanity chosen by God as the designated locus, moment and context for the fullest revelation of the
divine heart.

- The good news of Christianity amazes us by insisting that this revelation is still taking place in every single one of us, day in, day out.
The work of evangelisation is to provide us with the sacramental
vision to believe this, to find God's signature in every event of our
lives, God's footprints in every situation and experience that comes
our way, God's presence in all our comings and goings. There is no
exception to the truth of this revelation about the immanent holiness
of God's intimate energy. Perhaps nowhere more than in the heart-
felt dynamic of married life, where the human spirit stretches itself,
in its trusting and letting go, to the limits of its potential, is this
expression of incarnate love more clearly sacramentalised.

We discover, to our astonishment, that every ordinary human home
is the unexpected place where God dwells, whether this be recognised or not. Even where there is suspicion and deceit, married life
must remain an epiphany of mystery; a participation in God's own
challenging essence. Any time we say 'I'm trying to forgive you' or 'I
still believe in you' or 'I love you' to each other, is also the expression
of God's incarnate covenant within us, constantly healing and completing all that is imperfect. What a joy it is to be telling people about
this astonishing truth!

- There is an orthodox pedagogical approach that is appropriate for a
Catholic education inspired by the sacramental vision of a theology
of nature and grace. It is an approach based on life itself. It is incarnational in that it is based on the real lived experience of the students
themselves. Its aim is the transformed self-awareness of each student in the light of what Jesus did, of who he was, and of his continuing presence at the centre of our lives. This is what we call the
abundant life in the here and now. It is mediated through the essential traditions and practices of scripture, doctrine, the liturgy and the
life-witness of Christian saints and scholars. This life-theme
approach to the experience of redeeming, liberating grace is discussed in Part Three.

Two Liturgies

At the end of Part One we considered the liturgical celebration of the
earthy vision revealed in the incarnation as a central dimension of
Christianity. It reminds us of the presence of God in the midst of life.
There is a convincing reason for the Sunday Mass obligation. We so

easily forget the good news. The pervasive presence of original sin keeps blinding us to what redeems and renews us, to the precious potential of our humanity and of our world.

However, the whole meaning of liturgical celebration will be radically coloured by our theology of creation and salvation. We have already touched on this very important point. We noted that a sin/redemption-based theology will tend to focus on the quality and good order of the celebration itself, emphasising its intrinsic holiness, its distinctiveness and independence from created things; a nature/grace understanding will emphasise the truly sacramental nature of the celebration, pointing away from itself towards the already-holy humanity which it prays to purify and celebrate. It is, as we have seen, not always easy to hold them comfortably together.

Within this second emphasis it is helpful to refer to two further uses of the term 'liturgy' – the liturgy of the world and the liturgy of the church; the sacrament of the universe and the sacrament of the Mass; the table of our lives and the table of the bread and wine. In a theology of nature and grace they cannot be separated. If we are not in a holy communion with God's people in the routine lives we live, we will hardly experience an intensely divine intimacy at the Holy Communion of Mass. Theologian Karl Rahner, in *Secular Life and the Sacraments*, reminds us about the danger of seeing our participation in sacramental celebration as an end in itself. Unless our liturgy sensitises us to the presence of Christ in the person of our neighbour, it is, he insists, a 'worthless' preoccupation.

The liturgy of the world and the liturgy of the church; the sacrament of the universe and the sacrament of the Mass.

Fr Kevin Kelly writes: 'Today when people speak of the Real Presence they normally mean the sacramental presence of Christ in the Eucharist under the form of bread and wine. And when they speak of the Mystical Body they normally mean the church. For more than half of the church's history – that is, until the twelfth century – the very opposite was true. The "real" body of Christ was the church. And the "mystical" body of Christ was the sacramental bread and wine. We can see this usage in the passage from St John Chrysostom which Pope John Paul quotes in his encyclical on the Eucharist: "Do you wish to honour the body of Christ? Do not ignore him when he is naked. Do not pay him homage in the temple clad in silk, only then to neglect him outside where he is cold and ill-clad. What good is it if the eucharistic table is overloaded with golden chalices when your brother is dying of hunger? Start by satisfying his hunger and then with what is left you may adorn the altar as well".'[16]

The first aim in an authentic liturgical catechesis is, as we have been emphasising, to present the sacraments as of a piece with our lives in our world; to see them in the context of a world already permeated with God's presence, encompassed by divine love. In the very person of Christ himself, this intimate unity has taken place. The human is now the address of the divine, the raw material of our redemption. 'Salvation' wrote Tertullian, 'hinges on the flesh.' The art is to enable this revelation to be known and celebrated; to enable people to gladly accept and to become 'who they already are'.

To the more legalistic, calculating mind the notion of the sacramental imagination is too undefined and risky, too vague to measure, too unreachable to possess; to the contemplative mind it is the beckoning horizon of love and meaning that transforms the soul and enlightens the wavering heart. There is a functional paradigm of rubrical uniformity; and there is a liberating paradigm of life-giving worship. Many contemporary liturgists believe that our sacramental celebrations could do with the services of our best theatre-directors, and our teaching and preaching with the best of our poets, playwrights and actors!

We have already noted (in Part One) that Gregory Baum, a *peritus* at the Second Vatican Council, held that the liturgy is the celebration of the deepest dimension of human life, God's self-communication to all humanity. 'Liturgy' he wrote, 'unites people more closely to their daily lives. Worship remembers and celebrates the marvellous things God works in the lives of human beings, purifies and intensifies these gifts, makes everyone more sensitive to the Word and Spirit present in their daily lives.'[17]

> If we find no hint of divine immanence in the emotions and experiences of our lives, then, it is highly unlikely that we will touch the closeness of God at the liturgical assembly.

The liturgy, 'the work of the people' can never afford to lose its moorings in the anchorage of their lives. The celebrant and pastoral liturgical team will be deeply familiar with the significant moments in the life of the parish and its parishioners. Then all kinds of things – the beauty, goodness, tragedy of our lives – can be a compelling opportunity for the disclosure of the presence of God to be recognised and high-lighted, where appropriate, in the liturgies.

That is why liturgy has such a potential for transformation. We have already noted that in a homily shortly after his inauguration, Pope Benedict called for a greater sense of beauty in achieving this promise. 'If the church is to continue to transform and to humanise the world, how can she dispense with beauty in her liturgies, that beauty which is so closely linked with love, and with the radiance of the Resurrection?'

Two Languages

The sensitive care in the preparation and celebration of the liturgy that Pope Benedict desires, applies too to the language we use in all presentations of the good news. Too often we settle for mediocre ritual and obsolete phrases to convey a glimpse of the unutterable beauty of Christian revelation, of the astonishing fact that God loves us so dearly. Only the best language is good enough to reflect God's compassionate heart. No effort is spared in crafting a love-letter. Spiritual writers and speakers have taken endless pains to get the weight and texture, the shape, sound and rhythm of their words as perfect as can be. They believe that since God, and the things of God, are at the heart of our lives, then we should create the most beautiful ways of speaking and writing about the Gracious Mystery.

It is such an exquisitely delightful thing to be doing – to be waking up the hearts of young and old to the reality of how beautiful they are, and how extravagantly desired they are by a Tremendous Lover. Increasingly, across the world, theologians speak of the need for a poetic, lyrical and attractive language and imagery for spreading the amazing revelation – that there's no part of our lives or world that isn't already everlastingly graced and blessed by God's beauty. What is needed, they agree, is a language that touches the heart.

Theologians speak of the need for a poetic, lyrical and attractive language and imagery – a language that touches the heart.

This applies especially to the ministry of spreading the gospel. This work is profoundly sacred. You don't, for instance, let just any old interior decorator loose on the Sistine chapel to restore and reveal the exquisite details of its breath-taking beauty. Only the best in the world will do for such ultra-special work. We, too, need to test and filter every expression we use to make sure that the language is fresh, relevant and true to the original revelation of God in Jesus. We need to look at the ideas and insights of our best theologians, educationalists and poets, past and present, to make sure we are not short-selling that captivating story that God wants every human heart to hear.

It was probably never more difficult to communicate meaningfully than it is today. Here again in our calling to evangelise, we need to replace an outdated language with a more appropriate one. How do we ensure that the 'sacramental vision' of a reclaimed 'Catholic humanism' will engage with the crisis of communication – of translation, transmission and relevance – probably the greatest current challenge for a multi-cultural, postmodern Catholic inner-city parish or school today? We have noted already the question asked by theologian Fr David Power: 'How can we, in a time of computerisation and remote control, get beyond the stranglehold that technique and concept have on language, so that it may speak "in, with, and under" bread, wine, oil and water, through a poetics that allows the things themselves to come to speech, and through them, the gift of divine love and divine life that Jesus and the Spirit have poured into them?'[18]

In general terms, then, what would a concept of spirituality, or of evangelising look like in a highly technological, multi-religious, deeply pluralistic age? This is a huge concern and challenge. Our best prophets struggle with the way forward. It is worth recalling again the observations of John O'Donoghue quoted earlier. He believes that people need to be put in touch with their inner sense of wisdom and wonder.

> He emphasises that the good news is already within, and rises from, the true well at the centre of all life. 'This is the news that life itself is the primal sacrament; that life is the home of the eternal, albeit in veiled form; that the life of each person is a sacrament, wherein the eternal seeks to become visible and active; that each individual is chosen for a creative destiny in this world; that each one incarnates a different dimension of God; that at death, life is not ended, but elevated and transfigured into another form; that we are not outside, but within, God.'[19]

It is this kind of sacramental vision into the love and meaning already at the 'well of life itself' that will bring a new insight and courage to the work of evangelisation. We have already noted Vincent Donovan's remark of many years ago that we do not bring God to people: 'We awaken the presence of God in them. This is the heart of the spiritual journey, to bring that presence to awareness. This is a delicate and sensitive work. Awareness cannot be forced; it can only be awakened.' A tentative definition of evangelising might see it as bringing to consciousness in people a sense of God's presence within them; an awakening of people's slow awareness of who they really are. It is this awareness then that motivates a passion within us to relieve the poverty and pain of a world for which we are all, by virtue of our birth and baptism, forever responsible.

Compassionate Listening

This 'Endword' has already referred to the two theologies that give rise to differing approaches. The central thrust of *Begin with the Heart* draws attention to the inevitable connection between our modes of evangelising, catechising, celebrating liturgy and preaching on the one hand, and, on the other, the theological vision we hold as most accurate and inspiring. There is much matter for reflection here. It is so important to provide opportunities for catechists and teachers to mull over these matters, to come to grips with the underlying theological reasons supporting the catechetical guidelines and religious syllabuses they are given.

Much space has been devoted in Part Three of the book to the perennial debate about the nature of the content of catechesis and religious education. In some dioceses in these countries there has been a lessening of the cognitive dimension of catechesis in favour of a more subjective and affective emphasis. In others, the clear emphasis has been on the former. However, beyond more teaching and knowledge about God, it is widely held that what people long for now is the actual experience of God in their daily lives. This is probably the way it has always been.

What people long for now is the actual experience of God in their daily lives.

Writing about 'doing theological reflection' Dr Krisak of Loyola College holds that the scriptures reveal a people who saw the world around them in a new and sacramental way – a way that changed the way they experienced their own lives because of the way they had experienced God in their relationship with Jesus. 'We do not so much get an account of the identity of God from the scriptural texts,' he writes, 'as a view of the experience of God through the eyes of a believing people.'[20] The author explains that when we truly 'hear' the texts of scripture we enter into a new time zone which is about the daily possibilities for opportunity – endless opportunities for becoming participants in the unfolding and the present experiencing of the Loving Mystery we call God.

There are many opinions and questions around among catechists and RE experts about how the faith is 'passed on'. Is it to be learned or experienced? Is it to be taught or caught? Is it an individual achievement or does it happen only in community? How do you teach a 'vision'? How is the Catholic imagination again restored to our faith? There are arguments and syllabuses that favour a more formal, cerebral and factual approach and those that believe in a more life-changing and experience-centred approach. It is rather simplistic to sum it up as a matter of head versus heart. Without both dimensions of knowing and feeling, our growing and our being will be flawed and stunted. It is more about balance and emphasis.

It is a pity when differing views are expressed aggressively as though coming from opposing camps. As Roman Catholics, at least regarding these issues, we are not famous for compassionate listening. But this is something we need to start doing without delay. We are at some kind of turning-point in the faith-story of the church today. If our people are to find their voice and be heard again, if our church is to be greened and bring nourishment again, the there is a pressing need for humble and courageous conversations to begin immediately. *Begin with the Heart* is offered as a possible way in to a renewed sacramental vision of the Good News that is saving the world. Heart and head together – of course. But, begin with the heart!

Summary

There is a need to be confident about the model of theology on which our educational efforts are based.

The humanity of Christ is at the heart of all our 'humanising and transforming' work with others. (Benedict XVI)

God became human so that human beings could realise their divinity.

Original sin blinds us to the life-giving truth about our origin and destiny.

Recovering the language of love and excitement is the work of education.

There is a need, among catechists, to nourish their own deep awareness and experience of the freedom of sons and daughters of God.

That is the transforming experience that is 'caught' from the catechist and teacher.

 Courageous Conversations

How does our growing awareness of the way society is changing, lead to a re-visioning of our approaches to Christian education in all its forms?

Can we recognise God in all aspects of culture and other religions today?

How do our shared stories affect our understanding of being Christian?

What are the signs of a moral loneliness in the lives of many religion-less young people today?

What is so attractive, so invisible, yet so ambiguous and subtle in contemporary culture, in today's postmodern society?

Does our maturity, our personal responsibility, match today's culture of freedom?

What are the obvious indications of our current individualisation, our loss of a sense of the common good, of community?

Would themes such as 'desire', 'freedom' and 'belonging' form a common ground for 'conversation' in a pluralist context?

Do we realise the extent and the challenge of the changed face of the society we now belong to? (Karl Rahner's comment: 'Never take for granted that everyone alive at the same time belongs to the same generation.' And, how many generations, cultures, beliefs are there in one RC inner-city Secondary School?)

What are the advantages and dangers in welcoming, rather than in condemning, the inevitable environment of a postmodern world? What are the challenges and opportunities it offers to Catholic Christianity to critique and purify itself?

How does our growing awareness of the way society is changing lead to a re-visioning of our faith and an exploration of how we present it to a new world?

How can the Catholic Church provide an authentically Christian postmodern spirituality and a postmodern catechesis for today's postmodern society?

Can you distinguish, in your own way of catechising and teaching, the two strands and strains (e.g. of head and heart) outlined in the final sections of *Begin with the Heart*? Would you agree that this is a huge issue facing the teaching church today? How would you suggest they can be woven into the one catechetical fabric?

Glossary

Catholic Modernity
Catholic modernity is an alternative vision of the modern age, understanding reality as bathed in grace and so, intrinsically open to God. Consequently, through this sacramental vision of reality, human existence is understood in the light of a Christian humanism; understanding the human as the image of Christ.

The vision proposed by OTWTL is a Catholic modernity with a sacramental heart. This begins with the acceptance of the true relationship between nature and grace, and includes a holistic language for communicating all that the church proclaims and that its presence creates.

Culture
The ideas of a particular civilisation at a particular time. A system, or systems, of shared beliefs, values, customs, behaviours and artefacts that members of a society or group use to interact with each other. These systems are transmitted from one generation to another through processes of learning and adaptation. The meeting place of the dialogue between the church and the contemporary culture it inhabits and is formed by, is a rich sense of humanity on the part of both partners in the dialogue.

Dualism
Dualism denies the intrinsic value of the created order, that all created things are good. There is no conflict between soul and body, between grace and nature, as though they were separate components, the one higher and the other lower. Holiness is wholeness. There is no 'secular' realm from which God is absent. The divine presence in the world may be hidden and even denied, but God is everywhere. Dichotomies between religion and life, between sacred and secular are false. The real distinction is not between grace and nature but between what is real and what is illusory, between a life lived in the truth of love and a life based on a false selfishness. Incarnation marks the end of any opposition between the spiritual and the earthly, transcending our fallen human tendencies to divisiveness. Our hope is for the salvation of the whole being, of all creation.

Modernism
The late 19th and 20th century movement that sought to promote both technological advance and experimental forms of art, literature and architecture. The movement was characterised by the use of unconven-

tional subject matter and style, and experimental techniques of expression. It was inherently optimistic and followed a belief in progress. In the Roman Catholic Church there were movements, at those times, that attempted to adapt church teachings to take account of modern scientific and philosophical thought.

Relativism

Any of various philosophical attitudes holding that moral value, knowledge or truth is not absolute but relative, for example to an individual, historical circumstances, or a theoretical framework. Relativism asserts that what may be true or rational in one situation may not be so in another. Such an approach offers great challenges to the churches. As usual, there is room for dialogue. In a postmodern age not all relativism is detrimental to religious faith.

Sacramental Imagination

The term 'imagination' is used throughout the Project in the sense of the power to reconfigure reality by seeing it through an alternative lens, acquiring a new vision of its graced character. The 'sacramental imagination' is a way of perceiving and understanding the reality of the world and the circumstances in which we live that makes Christ the key. It is the fruit of faith that perceives God at work in all created reality, especially in human life and relationships, so that they carry the image of Christ. This use of imagination in theology is far removed from mere fantasy or artistic creative power. The sacramental imagination has its source in the incarnation. The retrieval and development of the sacramental imagination not only brings considerable coherence to the Catholic vision and process of religious education, catechesis and formation but it opens up new generative resources for engagement with contemporary cultures. (OTWTL)

Secularisation

The view that religious consideration should be excluded from civil affairs and public education. Secularism works towards the gradual confinement of religion to the private sphere and, in some interpretations, to its eventual elimination altogether. (OTWTL) The term indicates the belief that society's values and standards should not be influenced or controlled by religion or by the church. This relegation of matters religious to the margins of life arises from a sceptical indifference, or even open hostility, that is a real and growing threat to the role of Christianity in the world today. There is little evidence, as yet, of any serious desire for a mutual and mature encounter to search for a better understanding.

Theology of Nature and Grace

Grace has never had one single, agreed meaning in Catholic theology. Thomas Aquinas described the function of grace as both the healing of human nature wounded by sin, personal and original, and as the elevating of human nature to participation in the divine life. A theology of nature and grace and a theology of sin and redemption work together in Aquinas' understanding of incarnation. 'Grace builds on nature' he wrote. Grace elevates and transforms human nature, but human nature retains all its weaknesses. Grace presupposes nature; it does not replace it. Nature, too, supposes grace to the extent that the grace of Christ sustains us in our very human existence. Human existence is already graced existence. It is always unmerited and pure gift. Intrinsic to ordinary, everyday human experience, it is universally available. Since human existence is social as well as individual, grace has a social as well as an individual dimension. It radically transforms the whole created order.

Postmodernism

Postmodernism is a diverse movement that developed after the Second World War. Among its dominant features is a belief that all human knowledge is limited and culturally conditioned. It tends to refer to an intellectual state without a central organising principle. It carries extreme complexity, diversity and ambiguity. There is no way to stand outside discourse, it believes, so as to find objective truth such as revealed faith. Generally accepted stories (or 'meta-narratives') about knowledge, the world, God, no longer work to legitimise truth-claims. Instead, since the idea of reality and rationality is a cultural construct postmodernism celebrates a world of ever-changing meanings and relationships between things.

178

Notes

PART ONE

1. Gallagher, Michael Paul, *Retrieving Imagination in Theology* in *The Critical Spirit*, Pierce, A. and Smyth, G. eds (Columba 2003) p 207.

2. Rolheiser, Ronald, *A Mystical Imagination* ('Last Word' art in *The Catholic Herald*)

3. Hanvey, James and Carroll, Anthony, *On the Way to Life: Contemporary Culture and Theological Development as a Framework for Catholic Education, Catechesis and Formation* (OTWTL) A Study by the Heythrop Institute for Religion, Ethics and Public Life 2005. p 40.

4. ibid, p 40.

5. ibid, p 41.

6. Rolheiser, Ronald, *Beauty as God's Language*, op.cit., 12 September 2004.

7. OTWTL p 65.

8. ibid, p 66.

9. ibid, p 66.

10. ibid, p 63.

11. ibid, p 39.

12. Power, David N., *Sacramental Abundance* (*The Way Supplement* 1999/94) p 90.

13. Interview with Seamus Heaney (*Irish American* May/June 1996) p 28, quoted in *Sacramental Abundance*, op. cit.

14. John Paul II, *The Place Within: The poetry of Pope John Paul II*, (Hutchinson 1995).

15. Cowper, William, *A Winter Walk at Noon* in the *Poetical works of William Cowper* (Oxford University Press 1934).

16. Moore, Thomas, *The Re-enchantment of Everyday Life* (Harper Perennial 1997) p 304.

17. ibid, p 314.

18. Greeley, Andrew, *The Catholic Imagination* (University of California Press 2001) p 170.

19. O'Donoghue, Noel D., *The Mountain behind the Mountain* (T and T Clark 1993) p 61.

20. ibid, p 29.

21. Gibran, Kahlil, *The Prophet* (Alfred A. Knopf 1977) p 28

22 Greeley, Andrew, op. cit. p 2.

23. ibid, p 7.

24. ibid, pp 173 *seq.*

25. Grey, Mary, *Sacred Longings: Ecofeminist Theology and Globalization* (SCM Press 2003) p 86.

26. Greeley, Andrew, op. cit. p 46.

27. Dillard, Annie, *Pilgrim at Tinker Creek* (HarperPerennial 1974) pp 33, 34 quoted in *Sacred Longings,* op. cit.

28. OTWTL, p 66.

29. Rahner, Karl, *Secular Life and the Sacraments – Part 2 (The Tablet* Vol 225, 1971⁾ p 267.

30. Baum, Gregory, *Man Becoming* (Herder and Herder 1973) p 75.

31. Hillesum, Etty, *Letters from Westerbrok* (Pantheon Books 1986) 71 quoted in *Sacred Longings,* op.cit. p 169.

32. Roccasalvo, Joan L., *Hans Urs von Balthasar: Theologian of Beauty* (The Way Oct 2005) p 60.

PART TWO

1. Rahner, Karl, *Theological Investigations Vol IV* (Darton, Longman and Todd, 1964) p 213.

2. McBrien, Richard, *Catholicism* (Geoffrey Chapman, 1994) p 266.

3. Rahner, Karl, *Secular Life and the Sacraments (The Tablet,* Vol 225, 1971) p 237.

4. OTWTL, p 39.

5. ibid, p 41.

6. ibid, p 66.

7. Rahner, Karl, *Secular Life and the Sacraments,* op. cit. p 237.

8. Lavery, Hugh, *Why Sacraments?* (Uniscripts No 9; Upholland Northern Institute 1978) p 1.

9. Vatican II Documents: *The Church in the Modern World,* para 22.

10. McBrien, Richard, op. cit. p 10.

11. Gilkey, Langdon, *Catholicism Confronts Modernity* (Seabury Press 1975) pp 17, 18, 20, 21 quoted in McBrien, op.cit.

12. John Paul II, *The Holy Spirit in the Life of the Church and of the World,* art 50.

13. John Paul II, *Ecclesia de Eucharistia,* p 1.

14. Lane, Dermot A., *The Experience of God* (Veritas 1985) p 3.

15. Ibid, p 29.

16. Ibid, p 71.

17. Rahner, Karl, *Foundations of Christian Faith: An Introduction to the Idea of Christianity* (Seabury Press 1978) p 131.

18. Kelly, G. B., *Karl Rahner: Theologian of the graced search for meaning* (T and T Clark 1993) p 100.

19. Rahner, Karl, *Nature and Grace: Dilemmas in the Modern Church* (Burns and Oates 1964) p 127.

20. Vatican II Documents, op.cit. para 22.

21. Fransen, Piet, *Divine Grace and Man* (Mentor-Omega 1965) pp 173, 174.

22. Rahner, Karl, *Secular Life and the Sacraments*, op. cit. p 237.

23. Mackey, James, *Grace* (art in *The Furrow*, Vol XXIV, 1973) p 341.

24. Fagan, Sean, *Sacraments in the Spiritual Life* (*Life and Doctrine*, Vol 23, No 8, 1973) p 40.

25. De Chardin, Teilhard, *Le Milieu Divin* (Collins 1960) p 59.

26. Schillebeeckx, Edward, *Christ the Sacrament* (Sheed and Ward 1963) pp 246, 247.

PART THREE

1. OTWTL, p 69.

2. Bruner, Jerome, *Process of Education* (Harvard University Press 1961) p 98.

3 Maritain, Jacques, *Education at the Crossroads* (Yale University Press 1943) p 9.

4. Himes, Michael, *Communicating the Faith: Conversations and Observations* in Imbelli, Robert, ed, *Handing on the Faith* (Crossroads Publishing 2006) p 114.

5. Cowper, William, op. cit.

6. Rohr, Richard, *Things Hidden; Scripture as Spirituality* (St Anthony's Press 2008).

7. O'Donoghue, Patrick, *Fit for Mission? Schools* (Diocese of Lancaster 2007).

8. Himes, Michael, op. cit. p 122.

9. O'Connell, Seamus, *The Menu is not the Meal* (*The Furrow*, Feb 2008).

10. O'Conaill, Sean, *Love before Knowledge* (*The Furrow*, June 2005).

11. Stock, Marcus, *Christ at the Centre* (Archdiocese of Birmingham 2005).

12. Strange, Roderick, *In the Spirit of Faith* (*The Tablet*, 8 April 2006).

13. Stevens, Wallace, *Palm at the End of the Mind: Selected Poems and a Play* (1972) quoted in Gallagher, M. P., op. cit.

14. OTWTL, p 63.

15. Kasper, W,. *An Introduction to Christian Faith* (Burns and Oates 1980) p 27.

16. Brooks, Geraldine, *Year of Wonders* (Fourth Estate 2002) p 235.

17. Conway, Eamonn, *Tales of Accidental Theologians* (*The Furrow*, Jan 2006) p 54.

18. Vatican II Documents: *The Church in the Modern World*, 4.

19. ibid, 1.

20. *On The Threshold: The Report of the Bishops' Conference Working Party on Sacramental Initiation* (Matthew James Publishing 2000) p 16.

21. ibid, p 12.

22. OTWTL, Introductory Material, p 13.

23. Vanstone, W. H., *Love's Endeavour, Love's Expense* (DLT 1977) p 70.

24. Goldby, M. *et al* (eds), *Curriculum Design* (Croom Helm 1975) p 477.

25. ibid, p 67.

26. OTWTL, p 65.

27. Clegg, Alec, *Loaves and Hyacinths* in *About Our Schools* (Basil Blackwell 1980) During the 70s and 80s there were great debates about the nature of spirituality, religion, religious experience and religious education in the Church of England. For an excellent summary of the major contributions of this period see Wright, Andrew, *Spiritual Pedagogy: A Survey, Critique and Reconstruction of Contemporary Spiritual Education in England and Wales* (Culham College Institute 1998) The author has written a very accessible and handy summary of his work on 'Teaching Spirituality' in his *Discerning the Spirit* (Culham College Institute 1999).

28. Nichols, Vincent, From an address to Headteachers on Spiritual and Moral Development and the Catholic School, London 1993.

29. Doran, R. and Crowe, F., eds, *Collected Works of Bernard Lonergan: Topics in Education* (Toronto 1993) p 217, quoted in Gallagher, Michael Paul, *Retrieving Imagination in Theology*, in *The Critical Spirit*, op. cit. pp 203,204

30 McCosker, Philip, *Blessed Tension: Barth and von Balthasar on the Music of Mozart* (*The Way*, Oct 2005) p 91.

31. Congregation for Catholic Education, 1977.

32. Wordsworth, William, *The Prelude*, Jonathan Wordsworth, ed, (Penguin 1995) Bk 14, 11, 446-47 quoted in Himes, Michael, op.cit.

33. Van Doren, Mark, *Mark Van Doren: 100 Poems* (Farrar, Straus and Giroux Inc, 1967).

34. De Mello, Anthony 'The Explorer' in *The Song of the Bird* (Anand Press 1982) quoted in Conway, Eamonn, op.cit.

35. Conway, Eamonn, op. cit. p 56.

36. Grey, Mary, *Christian Theology, Spirituality and the Curriculum* in *Spirituality and the Curriculum*, Thatcher, A., ed,. (Cassell 1999) p 27.

37. Murray, Paul, 'Know Who You Are' in *The Absent Fountain* (The Dedalus Press 1991).

38. *Evangelisation in the Modern World*, 15.

39. *On The Threshold*, p 39.

40. *Catechesis in our Time*, 61.

41. OTWTL, p 66.

42. Groome, Thomas, *Forging in the Smithy of the Teacher's Soul* in Prendergast, N. and Monahan, L., eds, *Reimagining the Catholic School* (Veritas 2003) pp 35-45.

43. Barry, Carol, *Spirituality and the Educator* in Prendergast *et al.*, op cit. pp 46-55.

44. Parker, Palmer J., *The Courage to Teach* (Jossey-Bass 1998) p 2.

45. Tessimond, A. S. J,. *The Deaf Animal* from *Selection* (Putnam 1958).

46. Konstant, David, Address to Catholic Teachers' Federation, UK 1996.

47. *Evangelii Nuntiandi*, 41.

48. Congregation for Catholic Schools, 1977.

49. Bishops' Conference Statement on RE in Schools, 2000.

50. Kessler, Rachael, *Soul of Students; Soul of Teachers* in Lantieri, Linda, ed, *Schools with Spirit* (Beacon Press 2001) p 111.

51 Kessler, Rachael, *The Soul of Education: Helping Students find Connection, Compassion and Character* (www.mediatorsfoundation.org/isel)

52. Himes, M.; Ruddy, C. and D.; Tilley, T. W.; Groome, T.; Cupich, Bishop B.; in *Handing on the Faith; The Church's Mission and Challenge*, Part Three (Crossroad Publishing Company, 2006).

PART FOUR

1, Pierce, A. and Smyth, G., op. cit. p 25.

2. OTWTL, Introductory Material, p 12.

3. OTWTL, p 33.

4. McCarthy, Jeremiah J., *Theological Education in a Postmodern Era*, Paper presented at Wocati General Assembly, 2002.

5. Lash, Nicholas, *Holiness, Speech and Silence* (Ashgate 2004) pp 39, 40.

6. Endean, Philip, Foreword in *The Way* July 1996. (This issue, and that of October 1944, offer much insight into this debate.)

7. ibid, p 178.

8. Brady, Veronica, *Postmodernism and the Spiritual Life* in *The Way* op. cit. p 183.

9. Esteban, Rafael, *Evangelisation, Culture and Spirituality* in *The Way* Oct 1994 p 281.

10. O'Donoghue, John, *To Awaken the Divinity Within* in *The Way* op. cit. p 267.

11. ibid, p 268.

12. Rahner, Karl, *The Immediate Experience of God in The Spiritual Exercises of St Ignatius of Loyola*, quoted in Kelly, G., op.cit. p 56.

13. Rahner, Karl, *Dialogue: Conversations and Dialogues*, 1986 quoted in *The Furrow*, Nov 2005 p 630.

14. Ibid.

15. Lane, Dermot A., *New Century, New Society: Christian Perspectives* (Columba Press 1999) p 173.

16. Kelly, Kevin, *The Body of Christ* in *The Furrow*, September 2005, p 464.

17. Baum, Gregory, op.cit. p 75.

18. Power, David N., op. cit. p 90.

19. O'Donoghue, John, op. cit. p 267.

20. Krisak, Anthony, *Theological Reflection: Unfolding the Mystery* in *Spirituality for Ministers*, Wicks, Robert J., ed, (Paulist Press 1995), pp 314, 316.